EVERTON BLUES

Also by Neville Southall:

IN SEARCH OF PERFECTION

NEVILLE SOUTHALL

With *Ric George*

Everton Blues

A PREMIER LEAGUE DIARY

B&W PUBLISHING

First published 1997
by B&W Publishing Ltd
Edinburgh

ISBN 1 873631 75 8

British Library Cataloguing in Publication Data:
A catalogue record for this book is available
from the British Library

Picture credits:

The publishers would like to thank Empics,
Professional Sport International and
Everton FC for their invaluable assistance
with the photographs in this book.

Front cover picture © Professional Sport International
Back cover picture © Empics

Photo section:
Photographs of Paul Gerrard, the Everton Wall
and Paul Rideout © Professional Sport International
Everton Team Photo © Everton FC
All other photographs © Empics

Printed by WSOY

CONTENTS

ACKNOWLEDGEMENTS

I would like to thank Ric George
for putting the book together,
and also my thanks to David Prentice,
Paul Joyce and Terry Brennan
of the *Liverpool Echo*, and the
Liverpool Daily Post and Echo library
for all their help with
Everton Blues.

Neville Southall

PRE-SEASON

INTRODUCTION

The 1996/97 season won't be fondly remembered, either by myself or by Evertonians. It began, of course, with the usual optimism and genuine high promise, especially as some observers had named Everton as their Championship outsiders. Don't forget that we had finished sixth the previous year, only two points off a UEFA Cup place.

The least I can say is that things didn't quite go to plan. The word disastrous is, perhaps, too strong to describe our campaign. But it wasn't much short of that. Put it this way: finishing just two points off relegation with an astoundingly weak squad, coupled with two domestic Cup defeats by teams from lower divisions, meant we had a record which did not exactly match the ambitions set when we began pre-season training on July 15.

Worse still, our manager abandoned ship at the most crucial part of a turbulent season, leaving my future and, more importantly, that of the club, in doubt.

Let me just set the scene for you. When we all reported in mid-July, our only new recruit was Gary Speed, my Wales team-mate, who was signed from Leeds United for £3.5 million. It was thought a lot of money at the time, but I was pleased because we needed a goal-scoring midfielder and in Gary we got one with world class ability. People should never sneer at quality. I was sure Gary would prove his worth, and I'm pleased to say I was right, because he finished the season as our top scorer with 11 goals, nine of them in the League.

Morale is always high at the start of the season, and ours was excellent. Duncan Ferguson, for example, was flying in training. I have never seen him so fit. All the signs were that we were going to do well.

Understandably, our manager, Joe Royle, was looking for more reinforcements to fulfil the promise of the previous year. When I was approached to write this book, I hoped I would be recording a season of success. It gives me no pleasure to recall some of my experiences in what, I have to say, turned out to be one of the most eventful seasons of my long career.

I guess I should have been prepared for a tough time personally when, in July, the manager tried to sign Nigel Martyn from Crystal Palace. That was a bolt from the blue to me. Okay, I knew he wanted to buy another goalkeeper—a young one—as cover. But to go for some-one closer to my age was a bit of a shock.

I told the gaffer I didn't really give a monkey's who he bought, and that, good keeper though Nigel is, I didn't think he was any better than me. Not surprisingly, when the Martyn story broke, the papers were suggesting it could be the end of Neville Southall's Everton career. They had a point.

I had signed a new two-year contract the previous month in which there was a clause which allowed me to leave for nothing at 28 days' notice. It was subsequently taken out and replaced with a gentleman's agreement between Royle and myself.

I have been asked if I was happy when Martyn joined Leeds. To be honest, I wasn't bothered either way. Yes, Nigel's presence would have represented a challenge, but life is full of challenges, isn't it?

You see, when a manager buys a player it's like he becomes his property, and he has often been bought to replace someone. That's why I always knew the manager would play Paul Gerrard at some stage in the season because he was obviously looking to replace me.

Having failed to sign Martyn, Royle had paid Oldham £1.5 million for Paul, whom he knew well through working with him at Boundary Park. Fair enough. But it left me wondering who would be his first choice. Any fears I had that I was no longer wanted at Everton were confirmed when the manager told me Wolverhampton

Wanderers had come in for me. Royle's exact words were: "You may as well go and talk to them this afternoon because they're desperate to sign you!" That told me all I needed to know. With Wales playing World Cup qualifying games, there was no way I could afford not to be first choice at my club.

I spoke to Wolves, and they offered me considerably more money than I was on at Everton. When I told Royle the deal I had been offered, he asked me: "What would happen if we matched their wages?" Was that a hint that he wanted me to stay?

Wolves were wonderful to me, and if I had chosen to leave Goodison Park then I would have definitely signed for them. But the bottom line was that I love Everton. I wanted to play for them and I wanted to keep playing in the Premiership.

Gerrard's arrival signalled the end of Jason Kearton's days at the club. Jason is a nice lad, who had been my understudy for several seasons, and I am delighted he went on to enjoy success last season at Crewe Alexandra, where he won promotion to the First Division through the Wembley play-offs. Jason needed a break in his career because he didn't really get a chance to prove himself at Everton.

Don't forget that amid all this activity we were playing warm-up games in preparation for our opening Premiership fixture against Newcastle United on August 17. Our first was against Borussia Moenchengladbach at Anfield in the four-team Sir John Moores Tournament, hosted by ourselves and Liverpool, and also featuring FC Porto. We drew 2-2 with the Germans—Duncan Ferguson and Gary Speed got our goals—before going down 3-2 in the penalty shoot-out, where David Unsworth and Graham Stuart scored, but Andy Hinchcliffe, Gary Speed, John Ebbrell and Duncan Ferguson missed.

The following day we played Liverpool, who had lost to Porto, for third place. Nobody really wanted a pre-season derby because there is enough tension in the two League confrontations, and this one at Goodison lived down to all expectations as we drew 0-0. Fortunately it had been decided there would be no shoot-out this time. I suppose to preserve local pride and spare embarrassment.

Next we had a short trip across the Mersey to Tranmere, where we won 2-1 thanks to goals from Fergie and Andrei Kanchelskis. Then we were into August and up to Aberdeen for Brian Grant's testimonial. Andrei, Dave Watson and a Brian Irvine own goal helped us to a 3-1 win.

Paul Gerrard was given his first Everton outing at Wrexham, where we won 4-3, Andrei getting all our goals. He looked in great form. We concluded our pre-season programme at Birmingham City, and again we managed a 2-1 win, where "Diamond" Stuart and Fergie were our scorers.

True, we may not have set the world alight in these

matches, but let's not forget they were designed to build up fitness and form. What's more, the results were positive, leaving us quietly confident that they had laid the foundations for nine stable and satisfactory months ahead. Nothing could have been further from the truth. As you'll discover.

AUGUST

SATURDAY, AUGUST 17

Everton v Newcastle United
This is a marvellous day for me, as I celebrate my record 700th Everton appearance with a deserved and truly magnificent win over a Newcastle side which includes £15 million world record buy Alan Shearer. Before the game, I am presented with a watch by our chairman, Peter Johnson. It is a gesture I appreciate.

As for the action, this is without doubt the biggest game of the day in Britain, and Duncan Ferguson is in great form. He's even running about! We outplay Newcastle from the first whistle, Shaka Hislop having to beat away Gary Speed's early header after Andrei Kanchelskis had crossed. We are supposed to be underdogs in this match, but you wouldn't think it—considering the way we compete for every ball, and the attractive football we are playing. I think it's good we begin our games against a top team rather than against someone like Coventry, because against Coventry we would quite possibly have lost!

We take the lead after 28 minutes when Fergie uses his strength to barge into the area and is impeded by Steve Watson. David Unsworth scores coolly from the spot with a shot to Hislop's right.

Big Duncan creates our second goal six minutes before half-time as he leaps high to flick on Graham Stuart's pass for Speed to ram in a debut goal. Great stuff! I'm not troubled until just before half-time when I push over a Shearer header.

Most of our good stuff comes in the first half and, after dispossessing Steve Howey in the box, Kanchelskis manages to round Hislop, only for the Newcastle keeper to recover well and scramble back to save his shot.

We lose our skipper, Dave Watson, at half-time with a knee injury, which probably explains why we weren't able to add to our lead. "Waggy" is an inspirational figure. Without him we would struggle. None of our other players seem to have the same presence as him. Dave Watson, you see, *is* Everton FC. He leads by example—he is probably the fittest player at the club at nearly 35 years of age—and he covers up the mistakes of others, something which is not always recognised. Dave has more hunger and desire for the game than anyone at Everton, be they YTS players or other senior professionals. He has the respect of everyone at the club because he's willing to be hurt for the club. That says it all. I just hope his problem isn't serious because we need him.

But this is a day of celebration because we have out-played one of the best teams in the country and one, I'm sure, that will be challenging for honours. As for ourselves, I think we have a chance of coming close to winning the Championship. If we play this type of football throughout the season and are lucky with injuries, then we are as good as anyone else.

Everton 2 Newcastle United 0

Southall; Barrett, Watson (Short 46), Unsworth,
Hinchcliffe; Kanchelskis, Ebbrell, Parkinson,
Speed; Ferguson, Stuart.
Subs (not used): Rideout, Grant, Limpar, Gerrard.

Attendance: 40,117

AUGUST 21

Manchester United v Everton
Alex Ferguson calls Everton "Wimbledon with one or two good players," which annoys our gaffer. Well, with John Ebbrell as skipper in the absence of Dave Watson, we give the Manchester United manager plenty to think about in another excellent first half where Duncan Ferguson continues where he left off last Saturday. His 34th minute goal which gives us the lead not only represents the first time a visiting team has scored at Old

Trafford since December, 1995, it is also set to be one of the quality strikes of the season. Taking Andrei Kanchelskis' pass on the edge of the area with his back to goal, he turns and fires a powerful, rising left foot drive which gives Peter Schmeichel no chance.

Six minutes later, Ferguson is at it again, as he rises majestically at the far post to head in Andy Hinchcliffe's deep cross. As against Newcastle, we don't want half-time to come because we are playing some excellent football and we should be more than two goals up. Fergie is leading the line so well that he is making Alan Shearer look second class. When his mind is focused on football, Duncan is excellent, but when it isn't, he isn't. Shearer is more consistent than Duncan—or, rather, he probably will be when he settles in at Newcastle—and that is the only difference. Sure, Shearer will score more goals, but he's a different type of striker and those goals are welcome bonuses. But it's his consistency which has given him the edge over Ferguson, unless things change this season.

We are so in control that another three points and another prized scalp should be ours. The only thing which worries me is Dennis Irwin, who is causing us all sorts of problems down the right. But our bench aren't alert to that and they get things wrong tactically. I'm hoping Joe Royle switches Kanchelskis to the left wing to combat Irwin's attacks, but he doesn't. The consequences are that I'm forced to save from Ryan Giggs, but in the

69th minute none of us can do anything to prevent Jordi Cruyff scoring with a header. We know we will face an onslaught for the remaining 21 minutes, plus whatever referee Graham Poll adds on. Alex Ferguson always wants time added on if United aren't ahead, and he thinks I am trying to waste some during the second half. He is not happy. But what choice do I have? We are under the cosh and on these occasions a bit of gamesmanship is called for. Sorry, Alex!

Nine minutes from the end, Irwin goes on another run and fires a low cross which the unlucky David Unsworth turns into his own net. I'm furious, not with Dave, but with the fact that our manager has failed to spot the threat Irwin's been posing. Had he done so, then United wouldn't be level, and we'd be on our way to a win.

Despite United's pressure, we still manufacture two chances to snatch all the points. Firstly Fergie shoots too close to Schmeichel and then Gary Speed hits the side netting after Tony Grant puts him through. Mind you, we are fortunate not to be punished—in the 93rd minute, by the way—when Cruyff misses a good opportunity.

I'm sure Alex Ferguson feels he has seen one of the teams who can push his own all the way this season, but he won't be too liberal with his praise for us. After all, even though United have dropped two home points, this is a moral victory for them. I like Ferguson's football psychology: if you get a good result against United, you are lucky; if you lose to them you are a good team.

Ferguson is always speaking up for his players and his team, which is what a manager should do. I admire him for that. It's great public relations, but it's also great management. Ferguson does a fantastic job all round for Manchester United. He always gets the club in the papers and he never has anything bad to say about it. For him, United's product is always the best and that's the way it should be.

We would obviously have settled for a 2-2 draw at Old Trafford before we'd kicked a ball, but at the final whistle we are all very disappointed because we thought we should have won. Having said that, we are certainly not downcast—far from it. Our football is so good at the moment and our team spirit so high that I tell a friend that we will at least finish in the top six this season— and that he shouldn't be surprised to see us become champions. This isn't me being outrageous; it's a genuine feeling. Royle also says he feels Everton are the dark horses for the title. Great minds, eh?

Manchester United 2 Everton 2

Southall; Barrett, Short, Unsworth, Hinchcliffe; Kanchelskis (Grant 71), Ebbrell, Parkinson, Speed; Ferguson, Stuart.
Subs (not used): Limpar, Hottiger, Rideout, Gerrard.
Attendance: 54,943

AUGUST 23

Peter Johnson says the club plans to raise £15 million from a new shares issue. If the idea is to spend the money on strengthening the team, then players and supporters will be all in favour. But only the Board are in full possession of the facts.

AUGUST 24

Tottenham Hotspur v Everton
You would think that after the encouraging result at Old Trafford, not to mention our first day success, that the only changes Joe Royle would make would be those he has to. Not so. John Ebbrell and I are usually the first players out warming up, and when I tell him to get changed for the game at White Hart Lane he says he isn't playing! I can't believe this. How can the manager make Ebbo captain in the previous match and then make him substitute for this one? John isn't every supporter's cup of tea, but he's a player's player, who I always thought was appreciated by Royle. Sometimes, though, John is his own worst enemy because he doesn't say anything when he's left out. I expect this experience will prompt him to have a chat with the manager next week. I understand he has been left out because Joe wants us to play more football—which explains the

presence of Tony Grant, who is a more technical player.

David Unsworth is our skipper today on a pitch which is disgraceful for so early in the season. Parts of it are so thin that they remind me of John Ebbrell's hair!

Chances are thin, too, although Andrei Kanchelskis causes Ian Walker problems with a 30-yarder which is pushed away. Spurs don't pose much of a threat, and they are made even weaker in the first half when Chris Armstrong hobbles off. Good!

Craig Short is presented with the best opportunity two minutes into the second half when Graham "Diamond" Stuart picks him out at the far post. Craig is totally unmarked with the goal at his mercy, and I can't believe it when he heads wide. Don't ask me how. It's a diabolical miss.

Mind you, we nearly sneak the victory, with Walker touching Diamond's diving header onto the bar and Duncan Ferguson shooting at the Spurs keeper when clean through in the dying moments.

This is another game we should have won because we were the better team. Don't get me wrong—I think Tony Grant is a fine player, but we have missed John Ebbrell today. Joe Royle is talking about our great start to the season, which is fair enough because we have come through three tough games unbeaten. But I'm not some-one who loses touch with reality. We have picked up five points when, really, we should have had all nine. Now *that* would have been a great start. Being slightly cynical, you could say this "great start" amounted to just a game and a half.

Tottenham Hotspur 0 Everton 0

Southall; Barrett, Short, Unsworth, Hinchcliffe;
Kanchelskis, Parkinson, Grant, Speed;
Ferguson, Stuart (Rideout 75).
Subs (not used): Ebbrell, Hottiger, Branch, Gerrard.
Attendance: 29,696

AUGUST 26

Andy Hinchcliffe gets his first England call-up for the forthcoming World Cup qualifier against Moldova, and it's thoroughly deserved. Andy is someone who has matured since he became a father and he has suddenly realised that football is quite important to him. Now that he has a family, he has to feed it! He has always had tremendous talent; it's just that football hasn't meant too much to him. Or, if it has, he hasn't shown it. Andy is a funny guy, who likes a laugh. He likes to knock football—he pretends he's happy if a game is called off—but deep down I reckon he loves the game.

Glenn Hoddle is looking for a left-sided player because of injury problems and I don't think he could have chosen anyone better than Andy, who is as good a crosser of the ball as anyone. We are all delighted for Andy and I hope he is given a chance in Moldova.

AUGUST 31

Wales v San Marino

No problems here. Mind you, we didn't expect any! It's not often the Cardiff crowd has a glut of Welsh goals to cheer, and I think they'll have gone home pleased. Dean Saunders gives us the perfect start after only two minutes, before Mark Hughes and Andy Melville make us untouchable.

John Robinson and Hughsie again score twice in a minute and seeing as I've had nothing to do, I decide to give Tony Roberts a game in my place in the 72nd minute. Three minutes later Deano hits our sixth.

Wales 6 San Marino 0

Southall (Roberts 72); Bowen, Melville, Coleman (Taylor 81), Pembridge, Robinson (Speed 78), Browning, Horne, Saunders, M. Hughes, Giggs.

Attendance: 37,000

SEPTEMBER

		Pts
6	SUNDERLAND	5
7	LIVERPOOL	5
8	EVERTON	5
9	TOTTENHAM H	5
10	NOTTINGHAM F	4

MONDAY, SEPTEMBER 2

Waggy's hopes of a speedy recovery are dashed when he learns he requires a hernia operation which is expected to keep him out of action for a further five weeks. This is news we definitely don't want to hear—especially with a physical game at Wimbledon coming up.

SEPTEMBER 4

Everton v Aston Villa
I have more work to do in this game than in all of the others put together so far, which can't be right. We have no excuses because Villa are the better side and they deserve their win, which is secured in the 62nd minute when Dwight Yorke jumps above Earl Barrett and Craig Short to head down Fernando Nelson's cross for Ugo

Ehiogu to score. Yorke has a great game, running everywhere and dribbling superbly, shooting against the underside of the bar just before Villa get their goal.

I make saves from Nelson, Sasa Curcic and Savo Milosevic, which just shows how impressive Villa are away from home. They are so good that I would definitely include them among the title contenders.

Our form is patchy, and we miss chances. Tony Grant's through ball sends Andrei Kanchelskis away, and after Michael Oakes blocks his shot Duncan Ferguson heads the rebound against a post.

This result tells me something is missing from our side. We should have collected maximum points at Manchester United and Tottenham, but this defeat really puts things into perspective: two points from a possible nine as we slip down to 11th place.

League tables at this stage of the season are no indication of how sides are going to fare—Sheffield Wednesday, for example, have won four out of four and are top—but if we are going to claim a place in Europe, we can't afford to drop many more silly points.

However, we are not too downbeat. Yes, Villa gave us a lesson in football, but we have already proved we have the ability to give the best teams a run for their money. It's important we learn from this match and keep our self-belief because it will certainly be tested against Wimbledon on Saturday.

Everton 0 Aston Villa 1

Southall; Barrett, Short, Unsworth, Hinchcliffe;
Kanchelskis, Parkinson, Grant, Speed;
Ferguson, Stuart (Rideout 66).
Subs (not used): Limpar, Hottiger, Ebbrell, Gerrard.
Attendance: 39,115

SEPTEMBER 7

Wimbledon v Everton

There is something about Everton which always seems to allow sides who haven't won to end their barren period. Fortunately, having lost their first three games, Wimbledon beat Tottenham on Wednesday which should ease the pressure on us. Unfortunately it doesn't.

This is a nightmare day for us, which becomes the Neil Ardley show as he scores one goal and makes the other three.

Defensively we are shambolic, and we should have heeded an early warning when Jon Goodman burst through only to shoot over the bar. It takes us at least 20 minutes to get going and when we do, Duncan Ferguson is furious when he is not awarded a penalty after Chris Perry clatters him to the ground.

Just as we threaten to take control, we concede a ridiculous goal in the 33rd minute. We are all aware of the danger Wimbledon pose from set-pieces, but none of us could have imagined Ardley would score from a

40-yard free-kick on the left touchline. Everyone, including myself, stands flatfooted as the ball floats into the net. I am not happy with this goal, and I expect to be slaughtered in the Press for it.

I'm not the only one who doesn't play well at Selhurst Park. None of us come out of this game with much credit.

We are so sloppy that we give the ball away from our kick-off at the start of the second half, and almost immediately we fall further behind from a corner. Ardley sends over a cross which Marcus Gayle heads past me at the near post. How do we come back from this?

Joe Royle sends on young Michael Branch for Tony Grant in the 52nd minute to give us more pace and presence in attack. Michael, a promising 17-year-old striker, had replaced Anders Limpar on the bench for this game, and now he has a chance to make a name for himself.

Unfortunately, before he has a chance to make an impression, Wimbledon score their third goal, after I save from Robbie Earle. Once again Ardley plays the ball in, once again we don't know how to deal with it, and Earle scores with a header from close range.

Branch is looking lively—at least he's running about. That may sound awful, but you need your forwards to chase lost causes. He's doing well and at last there is an Everton reaction, with the Wimbledon goalkeeper, Neil Sullivan, touching Gary Speed's drive for a corner and then saving from Duncan. But as we push forward in search of what is a lost cause, we leave gaps at the back, and Wimbledon exploit one of them 17 minutes from time, when Efan Ekoku scores from Ardley's pass which splits our defence.

I'm hoping this defeat is a blessing in disguise; that it will give us a kick up the backside and enable us to reproduce the football we showed in our early games.

Wimbledon 4 Everton 0
Southall; Barrett, Short, Unsworth, Hinchcliffe;
Kanchelskis, Parkinson, Grant (Branch 52),
Speed; Ferguson, Stuart.
Subs (not used): Rideout, Ebbrell, Hottiger, Gerrard.
Attendance: 13,684

SEPTEMBER 8

Predictably, the Sunday papers blame me for our defeat yesterday. The gaffer has told me I didn't play that badly, but I know I did. I am my own biggest critic. I know when I have done well and when I haven't. I don't need journalists to tell me. I know how these people work; I could have written the headlines for them. I think they came to do me at Selhurst Park because I am Neville Southall, because I've made more appearances for Everton and Wales than anyone and because I'm approaching 40. That's cannon fodder for the Press. They need an angle for their stories, and so why not angle their reports on me? After all, they're not going to base their reports on Andrei not tackling back or Duncan not scoring, because that's not interesting enough. If you let four goals in, then it's only natural, I suppose, that the goalkeeper will come under the spotlight. But I can take the stick because I don't have too many bad games.

These days I am too long in the tooth to let headlines bother me. I am more prepared now for this sort of thing than I've ever been. I have to say, though, that the criticism was justified in this instance. The point I'm making is that there have been occasions when I have played well and still been hammered by the Press. Bless them.

SEPTEMBER 14

Everton v Middlesbrough
Michael Branch's performance at Wimbledon earns him a starting place and, at 17 years and 332 days, he becomes the youngest Everton player to figure in a first team match at Goodison. Ebbo is back, too, and we look quite comfortable in the first half. Craig Short, operating in a back three alongside Earl Barrett and David Unsworth, puts us ahead in the seventh minute by heading home Andy Hinchcliffe's cross when unmarked.

Juninho, one of 'Boro's Brazilians, shoots at my legs as the home team get back into the game, but I am more impressed by his compatriot Emerson. This guy looks a great player. He shows some brilliant touches and has great vision. He is a powerhouse of a player but with wonderful technique. Emerson reminds me of Bryan Robson—but with more ability.

Alan Miller saves from Andrei before half-time but, with Emerson taking control in the second half, Middlesbrough equalise just after the hour when Nick Barmby lobs over me after Derek Whyte's long pass is missed by our defence.

We respond well, with Whyte clearing off the line from Fergie, and Miller turning the same player's header for a corner. But Middlesbrough take the lead in style as Neil Cox plays the ball to Barmby, who back-heels for Juninho to sweep the ball home nine minutes from the end.

We press hard for an equaliser, but Miller again does well to save another Ferguson header. This win takes Middlesbrough into fourth place, just one point behind Manchester United, who have gone top. We are now fifth from bottom and I'm starting to get worried by the number of daft goals we are letting in.

Everton 1 Middlesbrough 2
Southall; Barrett, Short, Unsworth; Kanchelskis,
Parkinson, Ebbrell, Speed, Hinchcliffe,
Ferguson, Branch (Stuart 55).
Subs (not used): Rideout, Hottiger, Grant, Gerrard.
Attendance: 39,250

SEPTEMBER 18

Everton v York City
(Coca Cola Cup 2nd Round, 1st leg)
We appear to have problems when we play the so-called lesser teams and, true to form, we struggle against York. Less than 12,000 people turn up for this game, which shows you the appeal. Middlesbrough, for example, attract 17,000 for their game against Hereford—and they rattle seven past them.

That's not to say we don't make chances. It's just that the York keeper, Andy Warrington, is in top form. He makes a brilliant save from Paul Rideout's close-range header which would have won us the game, having earlier denied Gary Speed, David Unsworth and Andrei Kanchelskis, while being grateful to his defenders for making goal-line clearances.

We are stunned when Neil Tolson gives York a 55th minute lead. Fortunately it takes us just three minutes to reply, Andrei scoring with a fine left foot shot. York can be justifiably proud of their achievement, but at least we have the second leg where we can put things right. I know it will be hard for us up at Bootham Crescent, but we are capable of winning there because we have players who can counter-attack when York come at us.

We have to sort out this problem of being unable to impose ourselves against weaker opponents, and I don't just mean sides from outside the Premier League.

While I was highly optimistic at the start of the season, I'm now beginning to realise that we won't become champions because we are just too inconsistent. This problem has stared us in the face ever since Howard Kendall left.

I accept that the Coca Cola Cup doesn't have the appeal and the glamour of the FA Cup. If it was a straight knockout competition, played over only one leg, then it would be more exciting and more competitive. Unless it's a big tie, nobody seems to be interested in the early rounds. Motivation isn't a problem for me, but I think it could be for one or two of my team-mates. It looks as if we have players who can only play against top teams; they need the buzz from the big games. As far as I am concerned that's not good enough.

Everton 1 York City 1

Southall; Barrett, Short, Unsworth, Hinchcliffe; Parkinson, Ebbrell, Grant (Rideout 50), Speed; Ferguson, Kanchelskis.
Subs (not used): Stuart, Gerrard.

Attendance: 11,527

SEPTEMBER 21

Blackburn Rovers v Everton

No wins yet for Blackburn and they are playing Everton! But just when it seems we are going to be their first victims, we claw our way back to claim a point in another game we could have won. But it's another example of our not playing well against a mediocre side. Joe Royle makes changes, giving Paul Rideout his first start since January, and bringing in Anders Limpar for the first time since April because John Ebbrell has a hamstring injury.

Duncan squanders a good chance by shooting at goalkeeper Tim Flowers' legs, but we fall behind just after the half hour. Again it's another bad goal to concede because we just stand off and watch Georgios Donis run 50 yards from the halfway line past a couple of half-hearted challenges. It's a great finish from the Greek, but he should never have been allowed to get so near to our goal. We manage to equalise quickly, David Unsworth back-heading Andy Hinchcliffe's free-kick at the near post over Flowers.

Donis causes me problems with another shot in the second half, but we tighten up and create our own opportunities. Andrei shoots tamely at the Blackburn keeper but at least Anders makes him work after a powerful drive.

Sadly, three minutes from time, Big Duncan gets sent off for . . . stating the truth. I'll explain. He is annoyed that referee David Elleray has penalised him for fouling Colin Hendry and he is shown a yellow card for his protests. About a minute later, he continues to object and Elleray sends him off. So where does the truth come in?

Well, all Duncan did was tell the referee he was a baldy so and so. Elleray is bald, so what's wrong with that? Sorry, ref, but that's a nothing offence and it appears that Fergie has been sent off just for being Fergie.

Duncan is 6' 4" and so he can intimidate referees. Not by what he does but just by his physique, and that can count against him. He is fouled loads of times but he doesn't always get the free-kicks because he is such a big lad.

Just to compound matters, we find out after the game that Fergie is going to have exploratory knee surgery. It's been a good day for him!

Blackburn Rovers 1 Everton 1

Southall; Barrett, Short, Unsworth, Hinchcliffe; Kanchelskis, Parkinson, Speed, Limpar (Grant 88); Ferguson, Rideout.
Subs (not used): Stuart, Hottiger, Branch, Gerrard.

Attendance: 27,091

SEPTEMBER 24

York City v Everton
(Coca Cola Cup 2nd Round, 2nd leg)
When you mention The Shambles in York, people think you're talking about the quaint cobbled street in the city centre. If I happen to mention it there, I'm referring to our performance at Bootham Crescent. We are without

Craig Short, so Joe Royle brings Marc Hottiger in for his first start of the season and it's not a happy experience for him. Marc might have had a chance of starting the season had he not been injured, but I can't help thinking he's one of these "get them in, get them out" players. Hottiger is playing behind Andrei who, going forward, is fantastic, but he doesn't exist as a defender. Marc is so quiet, both on and off the field. He just gets on with life. He's been capped loads of times by Switzerland and is a proven international, so he is not useless. But I think he is being used by Royle. I think he was bought because the gaffer feared injury would end Earl Barrett's career and he needed another right-back. Marc is quite popular with the lads, but he is in danger of being labelled second-rate and this experience won't have helped him. It couldn't have been easy for him to come straight into a team whose confidence has been knocked and who were facing a banana-skin of a tie.

Hottiger is a good pro. You can't knock him for that. But maybe he needs to communicate more with the lads. Earl is a better defender than him—there's no doubt about that. Marc is better on the ball, but in the games so far we have needed the best defenders.

Even more incredible than Hottiger's name on the teamsheet is the appearance of Matt Jackson on the bench; the same Matt Jackson whom the manager had bombed after our FA Cup defeat by Port Vale last season.

York are 18th in the Second Division, and we can't

even win one of our two games against them. We even
take the lead in this one when Paul Rideout hooks in a
23rd minute volley, but things don't go to plan as Neil
Tolson equalises 12 minutes later. We are level at half-
time, but an Achilles injury to Rideout means Michael
Branch replaces him for the second half, putting in another energetic performance. It's not enough, though,
because Gary Bull puts York ahead after Paul Stephen-
son's shot rebounds off a post, and four minutes from the
end Graeme Murty adds to our embarrassment.

The 2,000 travelling Everton fans are angry, and they
have every right to be. They chant: "What the hell is
going on?" and I can tell you they are not the only ones
wondering that. I must have had 75 million touches of
the ball in this game because of the pressure we are
under. We are getting hammered. York's front two cause
us endless problems, and if they can do that then we
must be struggling. Gary Speed, from Branchy's miss-
hit shot, scores for us in stoppage time, but it's too late.
To be honest, we don't deserve to get a result out of this
one.

At the end I feel embarrassed and angry as we are
kept behind in the dressing room for 30 minutes. The
anger stems from our lack of passion and drive, and
for the first time since he was allowed to leave in the
summer, I wish we still had Barry Horne. If we hadn't
got rid of him, we would not have lost to York. This was
the type of game he relishes. Joe Royle has tried to

change our style this season, but it isn't working, and our squad is a bit thin, too. We need more players—desperately.

Mind you, our preparation for this match wasn't good. I was amazed to see the lads sitting glumly in the reception area of the hotel hours before kick-off. The reason is that we all had to check out of our rooms at a ridiculous time. Someone somewhere had messed up. How can footballers not be allowed to stay in their rooms until it's time for their bus to take them to the ground? That, I'm afraid, is down to a lack of professionalism, and I knew instantly we were on a hiding to nothing, even though it does not excuse our performance.

York City 3 Everton 2
Southall; Hottiger, Unsworth, Barrett, Hinchcliffe; Kanchelskis, Parkinson, Speed, Limpar; Stuart, Rideout (Branch 46).
Subs (not used): Jackson, Gerrard.
Attendance: 7,854

SEPTEMBER 28

Everton v Sheffield Wednesday
The day begins with the news that our assistant manager, Willie Donachie, has turned down the chance to be Manchester City's manager. City have approached virtually the whole population to find a new boss, but they wanted

Willie because of his coaching ability and not because they can't find anyone else. I'm delighted Willie is staying at Everton—everyone is. He is an excellent coach and I think he works well with our gaffer. I think he'd have slightly more problems as a number one than a number two. I don't think Willie would want to be a front man. He's quite a shy person as well as being a hard worker and a deep thinker.

The good news is continued with a much-needed win. We play well, too, aided by the returns of Craig Short and Ebbo, while Branchy has a great game up front. Andrei also comes to life, forcing Kevin Pressman into a good early save. Branchy wins us a penalty when he is fouled by Des Walker, but amazingly David Unsworth crashes his spot-kick against the bar. It's the first time he has ever missed one. Still, I'm not too concerned because we are well on top and Andrei scores his first Premiership goal of the season in the 16th minute when he drills home a low shot.

It's thanks to Pressman that Wednesday aren't further behind by half-time. He saves well from Andrei, is fortunate that Unzy heads straight at him when he has two players unmarked, and then Speedo shoots straight at him. A second goal is sure to come, and we get it in the 59th minute, thanks to Branch's brilliant turn on Dejan Stefanovic. He crosses and Graham Stuart heads home. Diamond then sees Pressman push away a shot and then the Wednesday keeper turns behind a stinging drive

43

from Kanchelskis. I, meanwhile, adopt the role of a spectator. I like matches like these.

It's good to see the lads respond so positively after the York defeat, and it ensures morale is high for our next fixture, which is a fortnight away because of international matches. Our win over Wednesday lifts us to 13th, but not even the presence of Liverpool in first place will stop me looking at the top half of the table.

This game was featured on *Match of the Day*, which I rarely watch. But because this was a good performance I switched it on, only to see Alan Hansen pummelling Wednesday's defence. Didn't he think for a minute that the reason they were so poor was that they were made to look like that? Where was the credit for Everton?

Everton 2 Sheffield Wednesday 0

Southall; Barrett, Short, Unsworth, Hinchcliffe; Kanchelskis, Parkinson, Ebbrell, Speed; Stuart, Branch.
Subs (not used): Hottiger, Jackson, Grant, Limpar, Gerrard.
Attendance: 34,160

OCTOBER

		Pts
11	DERBY COUNTY	10
12	SUNDERLAND	9
13	EVERTON	9
14	TOTTENHAM H	8
15	WEST HAM UTD	8

TUESDAY, OCTOBER 1

The newspapers are full of rumours about Andrei Kanchelskis being sold to Fiorentina. He told me on the bus back from our game at Manchester United that he fancied another season in England before going abroad to sample something else before he hangs up his boots. I don't know if there is any truth in the Fiorentina stories, but I get the feeling Andrei is getting a bit frustrated at Everton. And there are all sorts of rumours flying around about him. He has complained about our style of play in the past, looking to the sky and muttering "volleyball, volleyball." He is not a long-ball fan. He likes the ball played to him in certain areas. I don't think our style of play suits him. If he had gone to somewhere like West Ham, where they play more football and where there is less pressure, he could get away with playing one good game in four or five and he would probably have been really happy.

Don't forget that Andrei came to us from Manchester United, where he was used to winning trophies. We had won the FA Cup the season before we signed him and, like everyone here, he thought Everton were set to enjoy another successful period. Joe Royle certainly gave him that impression. In fact, Andrei said the gaffer had promised to build his team around him and his style of play. But he isn't seeing that. Andrei lost his head against Port Vale last season, and I don't think our defeat by York has increased our chances of keeping hold of him.

When he's on song he is so potent it's unbelievable, and he defends really, really well when he wants to. He can win matches on his own. He has done that for United and for us. It's just a question of getting him going.

I'd say Andrei is a typical Russian. This is not meant to be a derogatory statement. What I mean is that he has marvellous technical ability, but there are days when he just doesn't produce. Russia should have won several World Cups because of the talent their players have. It doesn't surprise me that they haven't, because if they don't fancy it, they just don't do it. I think it's just their culture.

Look at the Germans. Every one of their teams is methodical and they get results. The French play with plenty of flair but don't win as much as they should. But, like the Russians, they play the right way. English sides are said to be lacking in flair, but they make up for that with their attitude and durability.

Andrei can be the best player in the world when he wants to be. But if things don't go right then he tends to lose interest. I like him, and I get on with him well. Perhaps that's because, like me, he likes to have a moan now and again. I would be sorry to see him go because there is no doubt he is a quality player. And considering our need to strengthen our squad, I don't think we can afford to lose him. I don't think our supporters would be too pleased if he went, either.

OCTOBER 5

Wales v Holland
What's clear from this game is that Holland are still a force, and yet Dean Saunders puts us ahead in Cardiff after only 17 minutes. I'm having a busy time, and I'm pleased with the way I play, particularly the saves I make from Roy Makaay, Ronald De Boer, Clarence Seedorf and Philip Cocu. We manage to hold out until the 73rd minute when Celtic's Pierre Van Hooydonk, who had only been on the field for three minutes, equalises. Two minutes later he puts Holland ahead, and our morale dies. Then, in the 80th minute, Ronald De Boer heads Holland's third.

The Dutch coach, Guus Hiddink, says afterwards that I've played more like a 23-year-old than a 38-year-old. These are kind words, but I would much rather he'd said nothing and we'd won.

Wales 1 Holland 3

Southall; Bowen, Pembridge (Legg 65),
Browning (Jenkins 84), Melville, Symons, Horne,
Robinson, Saunders, M. Hughes, Speed.

Attendance: 37,000

OCTOBER 12

Everton v West Ham

We keep an unchanged team and we record two successive wins for the first time this season. I like playing West
Ham at home. Firstly, because I know there will be a
good game of football and secondly because they will
always give us chances. In short, they are a good home
side, but not so good away from Upton Park.

The first half is nothing to write home about, but we
manage to go ahead in the 13th minute through Graham
Stuart, who side-foots home Andy Hinchcliffe's cross.
Almost immediately we lose Joe Parkinson through injury, and John Ebbrell suffers the same fate at half-time.
Joe Royle takes the unusual step of pushing Earl Barrett
into midfield in the second half and Diamond almost
scores a second goal instantly, only this time he fires at
Ludek Miklosko.

I am waiting for West Ham to do something, and
when they do I have to say I am pleased with the save I
make from Iain Dowie's dipping volley. Later on, a

combination of myself and Hinchcliffe foil Julian Dicks before we go further ahead in the 77th minute. This is a well-made goal with substitute Tony Grant, Diamond and Earl exchanging passes down the left before Earl releases Gary Speed. His shot is too powerful for Miklosko to hold.

Then we seem to take our foot off the gas and four minutes from time Hinchcliffe brings down Hugo Porfirio in the box. As ever, Dicks blasts home the penalty. People say keepers have no chance with his penalties because of the power he puts in them. I'd love to save one, but that's easier said than done because Dicks is a good penalty taker. You have to give him credit for that.

Fortunately, his goal comes too late to alter the result and we move up to ninth. Liverpool are no longer on top, so things are looking better all round!

Everton 2 West Ham 1

Southall; Barrett, Short, Unsworth, Hinchcliffe;
Kanchelskis, Ebbrell (Hottiger 46),
Parkinson (Grant 14), Speed; Stuart, Branch.
Subs (not used): Limpar, Jackson, Gerrard.

Attendance: 36,571

OCTOBER 21

Liverpool v Everton—rained off!
Duncan Ferguson is still injured as we prepare for tonight's derby at Anfield. But we aren't too worried because we have got the better of Liverpool over the last few years and they, too, have injury problems. The rain has come down all day and on arrival at the ground we hear there will be a pitch inspection by referee Roger Dilkes. It's true the ball isn't bouncing very high during my warm-up, but I don't expect the game to be off. After all, there was more water on the pitch when we played at Goodison last season. But amazingly, Dilkes decides the game won't be played—just 45 minutes before it is due to start. That is absolutely disgraceful.

You'd think that with all the technology available these days, there would be some way of clearing water off the surface of the pitch. I think it suits both managers to have the game postponed, but I certainly want to play—I've spent all week preparing for this—and you can bet both sets of fans, some of whom have travelled from all over the world, want it to go ahead.

What hurts most is that just across the Mersey, Tranmere Rovers are playing their First Division fixture—in a more open stadium! You're not going to tell me that there is blazing sunshine above Prenton Park, just a few miles away. I don't understand all this. If the Tranmere game was also called off, then I'm sure the people already inside Anfield would have found it easier to accept Dilkes' decision.

Okay, because of the boggy Anfield pitch, you wouldn't get a game of pure football. But when do you ever see a Merseyside derby for the purist? Besides, the conditions would have added to the excitement. In years gone by there is no way this game would have been postponed.

The referee's reason for not giving the go-ahead is that he fears players could be injured. Wait a second: we are talking about a soft pitch here, not one that's bone hard. How come, then, that games are played in snow and freezing conditions? Very odd.

Well, there is one bright spot on a dull day—Andrei Kanchelskis is presented with the *Liverpool Echo*'s Merseyside Footballer of the Year award for the 1995/96 season at a special dinner. Andrei was brilliant last season, scoring 16 goals—all in the League—and for a winger that is a remarkable total. He hasn't really got going yet this year, but if and when he does then we'll give opponents far more to think about.

OCTOBER 26

Vinny Samways has sent a statement to the *Liverpool Echo* explaining that there is a rift between him and Joe Royle. The players all know this, of course, and the fans probably assume it. But now everyone is fully aware of Vinny's situation, and why he's not getting a game.

Vinny is a good skilful player, but his problem is he has only one way of playing: the Vinny Samways way. He can't change his style to suit the team, and nor will he. It's clear to us all that we are not the right team for him. We are playing in a way where we make our mistakes in our opponents' half. Vinny wants to keep the ball in our half. Mike Walker brought him to Everton and he did okay for him because Mike's style of football was different to the one Joe Royle wants. Under Walker, Vinny sat on the ball, passed it about when he had to and hardly went over the halfway line. The consequences of this were that we didn't get anywhere and we let a lot of goals in from mistakes which were made in our own half.

Vinny hasn't exactly helped himself at this club. When we went to Blackburn last month he was in the squad—which, I admit, is something of a rarity—and I think he was down to play. But he refused to travel because he said he had no clothes! He also said his head wasn't right. In his statement, Vinny said that he was not 100% fit to travel to Ewood Park and, on telling Royle that, the gaffer said he didn't want him to make the trip. I think Vinny is a bit upset that there seem to be no developments in a recent link between him and South-ampton. But I think what he is doing is a bit out of order because if you are picked to play, then you should play.

I mean, Vinny's gripe with Royle stems from not getting a game!

I don't share Vinny's view. Mine is that even if you hate your manager and even if you hate your club, you have a duty to yourself and your family, quite apart from the supporters, to go out and produce to the best of your ability.

I think money is also an issue with Vinny. I think the gaffer wants him to leave, but the rumour is that he won't go until he gets a large sum of money he is owed by the club. I can't blame Vinny for hanging on, but there is still that question of attitude. Vinny is on a four-day week here. He doesn't play Saturdays, he has Sundays off and he has Thursdays off, with the rest of the lads. Now that's a pretty good deal, don't you think?

Footballers should want to play every game they can. You can stuff all this "I'm tired this week," or "I've got a slight knock and I can't play." I hate all that. If people don't want to play for their club, then their club should stop their wages. It's as simple as that. I'm serious. After all, what are players there for? If they don't want to work, then why the hell should they get paid? If players are so unhappy at a particular club, then they should have the guts to say they want to leave. But they won't because they don't want to lose any money. You see, when you ask to leave you forfeit the right to have any outstanding money paid to you. But when a club wants you out, you are in a better bargaining position in that you can insist it pays up the remainder of your contract. This is the stumbling block with Vinny. I wonder if there should be some kind of arbitration for footballers in these situations. But then, I suppose agents would get involved and things would probably get messy.

It's been suggested that Royle doesn't like Vinny because he's a Londoner. I don't think there is a personality clash, because Vinny is quite popular with the players. I think our gaffer is annoyed because of what happened, or didn't happen, at Blackburn—and who can blame him? How can Vinny's head not be right for that game when he's had nearly four months to prepare for it? When, then, will it ever be right? If I was the gaffer, I'd be thinking that if he doesn't want to play for me there is no point in keeping him, and even if it cost me money I'd want him out of the door. That's easy for me to say, I know, because it wouldn't be my money which would pay him off, but an unhappy player does less damage to a club when he's no longer there. By doing this, a manager gives the firm message to everyone else that if anyone messes him about, they'll be out.

Vinny is technically right to do what he's doing and want his money before he goes. I can understand his position on this issue, but no way can I see why he doesn't want to play for Everton. Maybe he feels he's being used. If that's the case, then no doubt Marc Hottiger feels the same, but he doesn't refuse to play. Ebbo has also been used over the years and he's a great professional.

OCTOBER 28

Nottingham Forest v Everton
Because there is more than a spot of rain I'm half expecting the game to be called off after our Anfield experience! Actually, it has helped us not playing the derby, because we feel fresher and we are able to record a great win in really difficult conditions.

I've said in the Press and in my goalkeeping coaching manual, *In Search of Perfection*, that Nottingham Forest always keep the heating on in the visitors' dressing room to try and tire opposing players before the match. On this occasion they turn it off—and we collect three points. Coincidence?

Waggy is back in our defence, while youngster Graham Allen is named as one of the substitutes. We start very well with Craig Short heading Andy Hinchcliffe's corner firmly past Mark Crossley after only five minutes. Crossley also has to save from Gary Speed and Andrei Kanchelskis, who is put through by Tony Grant. In just 15 minutes, Tony does enough to make us believe that he has real potential.

This is a good, professional performance where we defend well and are really pleased with the night's work, particularly as it means nine points out of nine since the York debacle. If that's not reacting in the right way, then I don't know what is.

Forest seem short of ideas and they don't look happy.

I'm a great admirer of Dean Saunders, but I can't for the life of me fathom out why he is played wide on the right when he's a central striker. Why do managers stifle people's talents? The signs are that Forest could struggle if they are not careful.

Nottingham Forest 0 Everton 1

Southall; Barrett, Short, Watson, Unsworth, Hinchcliffe; Kanchelskis, Parkinson, Speed; Branch (Grant 75), Stuart.
Subs (not used): Limpar, Hottiger, Allen, Gerrard.

Attendance: 19,892

OCTOBER 30

At last a new arrival! We sign England international Nick Barmby from Middlesbrough on a four-and-a-half year contract for a club record £5.75 million. I have to say I'm a bit surprised because I'm not sure where he's going to play.

If he's going to be operating behind the front two, then it would mean losing a midfielder. But who? From what I hear, most people reckon Graham Stuart will be out, with Nick being played as a striker. That would be a bit harsh on Diamond, who has been a great player for Everton. With him being a southerner (which, incidentally, is why the lads call him Diamond—as in Diamond Geezer), I admit that when he came I wasn't sure how he would adapt up here. But he's been fantastic. He has a great attitude and his work-rate is phenomenal. He can play in a few positions and he's a good pro. You want people like that to succeed. You need lads like that in every club. But at least Nick's arrival will keep people on their toes. There is no doubt he is a good player. He gets in the England team for a start. I just hope he's played in the right position—wherever that is.

NOVEMBER

		Pts
6	CHELSEA	19
7	ASTON VILLA	15
8	EVERTON	15
9	SHEFFIELD WED	15
10	TOTTENHAM H	14

MONDAY, NOVEMBER 4

Everton v Coventry City
We had hoped to have big Fergie back, but a calf strain means he won't be able to partner Nick Barmby. It doesn't seem to matter as we attack Coventry non-stop in a first half where we create enough chances to wrap up all the points. Nick does well in his debut alongside Graham Stuart, who keeps his place at the expense of Michael Branch.

Nick has impressed me in training. He is like a miniature Peter Beardsley. He's also clever like him on the field, with good skill, and he's a good finisher. When Peter came to Everton he was five or ten yards ahead of the rest of us in his thinking. The team wasn't good enough for him and he was too brainy and visionary for us. I hope things won't be like that with Nick.

Against Coventry all the signs are positive. We murder them, producing no less than 23 goal attempts, and yet we score only once—from a disputed first half penalty by Diamond after Barmby's shot hits Kevin Richardson's hand. But if we're talking controversy, then referee Graham Poll has to be mentioned. You would think that an illegal shove by Noel Whelan on Craig Short would bring us a free-kick. Oh, no. Poll gives Coventry a corner. Ridiculous! Then Diamond boots the ball against Kevin Richardson's legs, and it goes out of play. Our possession? Wrong again. The decision again favours Coventry. Talk about getting the breaks, because Gary McAllister's drive deflects past me off Shorty and we find ourselves pegged back against the run of play.

We should be beating teams like Coventry at Goodison. Andrei Kanchelskis is shooting from everywhere, but his aim isn't good. Diamond and Andy Hinchcliffe also shoot wide, while Steve Ogrizovic saves twice from Nick. Okay, Coventry can point to a bad miss by Peter Ndlovu, but Shorty and Speedo strike the woodwork for us and there is no doubt who deserves all the points.

As with our fixture at Forest, this is a Monday night game, put back two days because of those nice people at Sky. I don't know whether they deliberately set out to inconvenience people, but they are certainly quite good at it. I hate Monday games for two reasons. First of all you get lower attendances than on a Saturday and secondly people have usually spent their money by Monday and they are budgeting for the week ahead. I think it's unfair to expect people to travel vast distances sometimes on a Monday night when they have to get up for work the next day.

If we must have Monday football, then they should feature clubs who aren't miles apart geographically. Then there's the kick-off time. Eight o'clock is too late. Ideally, we should just play on Saturday afternoons, as we used to, with Tuesdays and Wednesdays set aside for mid-week matches.

You can say that Sky should have the right to dictate when games should take place because they have poured millions into English football. I disagree. Football should always come first, not television. TV came *after* football and yet Sky are now running our sport. We now have the tail wagging the dog, and that's a dangerous thing.

Sky will introduce pay-per-view football on a regular basis. Don't for one minute think they won't. That means people won't be able to see matches unless they fork out a lot of money. Where's the decency in that? You only have to look at what has happened with Prince Naseem Hamed. If you want to watch one of his fights on telly you have to buy your satellite system, pay your monthly subscription and pay more on top of that. It's fine if you've got the money because it gives you the choice. But what if you don't have the money? Have Sky thought of that? And if they have, do they really care? All pay-per-view does is encourage people to go down to the pub and watch TV. I don't think we should be encouraging people to head to the boozer, do you?

Don't get me wrong: I don't hate Sky. They have offered us loads more channels, which is fine. What I, and other people object to, is the daft kick-off times for their football and the rubbish which is talked in between. These people may be "experts," but I reckon the public just wants to watch the matches. They don't need an hour's briefing beforehand.

Everton 1 Coventry City 1

Southall; Barrett, Watson, Short, Unsworth (Branch 73), Hinchcliffe; Kanchelskis, Parkinson (Grant 82), Speed; Stuart, Barmby.
Subs (not used): Hottiger, Limpar, Gerrard.

Attendance: 31,477

NOVEMBER 6

The club announces the sad news that one of it's finest ever players, Tommy Lawton, has died. Even though I've never met him, I know Tommy's reputation as an Everton legend—a wartime centre-forward who is mentioned in the same breath as the great Dixie Dean.

NOVEMBER 9

Holland v Wales

Not the finest day of my life in Eindhoven. Our manager, Bobby Gould, has said that in the absence of Barry Horne, who is injured, we would vote to see who would be captain. Vinny Jones won, but I really don't know how. Vinny has a lot of leadership qualities, and it doesn't bother me who is skipper. But I voted for Gary Speed because I think he would thrive on the extra responsibility. I thought it would be a choice between him and Mark Pembridge.

Bobby decides that for this game the best form of defence is attack and we go at the Dutch. The plan works well . . . for about five minutes. Then we are annihilated. Holland are so devastating that they would beat anyone on this form.

Holland deserve every credit for the way they play. They react to every rebound and totally outclass us, with Arsenal's Dennis Bergkamp helping himself to a hat-trick. Ronald De Boer, Wim Jonk, Frank De Boer and Philip Cocu are the other Dutch scorers. For the record, Dean Saunders gets our goal, but you can't even call it a consolation. I make 19 or 20 saves in what is by far the busiest night I've had as a professional. When I was 14 and playing in a man's league, I was used to letting in 20. But this is different. If you add the chances the Dutch have had to the seven goals they've scored, you can see we've escaped lightly. Imagine losing 27-0. That's a rugby score.

It really comes home to me tonight that as a footballing nation Wales have not progressed since I started playing for them over 10 years ago. The only advance we have made is that we no longer have winged collars on our shirts and that we all have the same kit, but I don't think we can call that sufficient progress.

We are still in a rut, and Bobby is going to get slaughtered in the Press after this defeat. Looking at it positively, this game could be a watershed. I would like to think the Welsh FA will tell Bobby to change the whole system, from top to bottom. Yes, this is certainly a sad day for Welsh football, but what an opportunity we have now to change it all.

Holland 7 Wales 1
Southall; Symons, Melville, Neilson, M. Bowen,
V. Jones, J. Bowen (Robinson 57), Pembridge,
Speed, Saunders, Hartson.

NOVEMBER 14

Joe Royle tells Marc Hottiger he can go if someone comes in with the right offer. I can't say that comes as a surprise. Marc needs first team football, not only to boost his international prospects, but also to ensure his work permit is renewed for this country because he is a non-EU player. For that to happen, he needs to play in 75% of our games. It's not looking too good.

NOVEMBER 16

Everton v Southampton
Another seven goal hammering in the same week! Fortunately I'm not on the receiving end this time as we put five past Southampton in the first half. Fergie is fit—he played 45 minutes of an 'A'-team game against Blackburn this morning—but he is named on the bench. We revert to a flat back-four for this game, with Tony Grant coming into midfield and Shorty dropping out of defence to substitute.

We go ahead in the 12th minute when Gary Speed releases Nick Barmby down the right, who side-foots the ball across goal. Andrei Kanchelskis can't connect, but Graham Stuart can. Nine minutes later we are two-up as Granty and Diamond combine, resulting in Andrei curling a shot past Chris Woods. Gary Speed swaps passes with Nick Barmby and scores from 20 yards just before the half hour, and two minutes later he heads home from close range.

In the 34th minute Andrei scores with a header as Woods misjudges Andy Hinchcliffe's cross. I feel sorry for Woodsy. He had just been brought back from the

States by Graeme Souness and hoped to resurrect his career in England, but this is turning into a nightmare for him.

I'm surprised how easy this is for us. Southampton are as hopeless as we are fantastic. Incredibly, Egil Ostenstand pulls a goal back just before half-time and then I make a save from Jason Dodd. Other than that, I've had absolutely nothing to do. In fact, there's no point in my continuing. We are so on top that I suggest to Joe Royle that Paul Gerrard might as well gain some Premier League experience by playing the second half. I think it would be a nice, comfortable, pressure-free debut for him. The gaffer is a bit taken aback, but he agrees to let Paul go on and he does well—he comfortably takes the only cross which comes near him!

Nick gets our sixth goal—his first for Everton—in the 57th minute by turning in Andrei's centre at the far post. Nick then sends Diamond away, but Woods saves. However, he is beaten again in the 71st minute when Hinchcliffe's corner is powerfully headed home by Speedo, who completes his hat-trick. I'm made up for Gary because, like me, he had been on the wrong end of seven goals in Eindhoven a few days earlier.

It just goes to show you what a strange game football can be.

Everton 7 Southampton 1

Southall (Gerrard 46); Barrett, Watson, Unsworth,
Hinchcliffe; Kanchelskis, Parkinson, Grant,
Speed; Barmby, Stuart.
Subs (not used): Ferguson, Branch, Short, Allen.

Attendance: 35,669

NOVEMBER 20

Liverpool v Everton

This is a game both sides can win, but neither of us is
good enough to do so. Liverpool lose Steve McManaman
with hamstring trouble after 17 minutes, but they bring
on Stan Collymore and we go a goal behind after 30
minutes. Earlier, Speedo has to clear Mark Wright's header
off the line and then I tip away a 25-yarder from Jamie Redknapp which brings Liverpool a corner. The danger isn't
totally cleared and when Redknapp crosses from the right,
Robbie Fowler bullets a header past me. We had spoken
about the importance of marking at corners, so it baffles
and angers me that Fowler is left unmarked on this one.

Liverpool go top of the table if they win this game,
which is an added reason why we must stop them. We
don't look inferior to them. In fact, at times we out-pass
them, which must come as a hell of a shock to them
considering the criticism they often throw at us for our
so-called physical approach. When we want to, we can
play some great football. It's just that we don't do it often

enough. I guess it's another case of our rising to the occasion. Newcastle, Manchester United and now Liverpool have all seen at first hand that we are fairly useful.

Joe Royle takes Andrei off at half-time because he is complaining of feeling ill. Mind you, he hasn't had much joy against Stig Inge Bjornebye. Big Duncan comes on and we suddenly become the better team even though I have to make a save from a Collymore header.

Speedo shoots tamely at David James, but I can sense an equaliser coming. We definitely deserve one, and it's Speedo who gets it eight minutes from time with a glancing header from Andy Hinchcliffe's free-kick. Liverpool find themselves in the unusual position of clinging on at Anfield as Redknapp scrambles the ball away from under the bar when Unzy meets Hinchcliffe's corner. Then, in the last minute, James saves from Fergie.

We have become something of a bogey side to Liverpool. Players like Joe Parkinson, John Ebbrell and Barry Horne have, over the last few years, tackled everything that moved, while, until today, Andrei has also turned on the style against them.

I suppose a draw is a fair result. I'm starting to like derbies because, touch wood, it's been a while since I've lost one. I'm also realising that because of my age I never know which will be my last. I'm trying to make the most of each one. In fact, I intend enjoying all my games this season because I feel with this manager the writing is on the wall for me.

Liverpool 1 Everton 1

Southall; Barrett, Watson, Unsworth, Hinchcliffe;
Kanchelskis (Ferguson 46), Parkinson, Grant,
Speed; Stuart, Barmby.
Subs (not used): Short, Branch, Allen, Gerrard.

Attendance: 40,751

NOVEMBER 22

Tony Grant signs a new four-year contract. Here we have a very promising youngster who, in order to fulfil his potential, needs an injury-free season in which he can play all the games. No-one can doubt his ability because he has fantastic skill and great vision. I know Andrei thinks the world of him because he reckons Tony is the only one here who can give him the passes he wants. At the moment Granty is like a bit-player when he should be an integral part of the team. But in order to become that he has to mature, firstly as a person and then as a player.

It's very noticeable that certain single lads at Everton are still immature in lots of ways. Perhaps Tony needs a steady relationship, where he gets married or has a kid or whatever, and matures. Andy Hinchcliffe, as I've already mentioned, is the prime example of someone who has matured after the birth of his child. It's only a thought.

NOVEMBER 23

Leicester City v Everton

Andrei's 'flu means a return for Duncan to our attack and automatically solves a selection dilemma for the manager. We know this will be a tough game because Martin O'Neill has already shown he can get the best out of his players. Leicester are holding their own so far in their first season back in the Premiership, when many people expected them to be propping up the table by now. They remind me of Wimbledon in many ways because they are quite physical and they know how to cause problems. Also, like Wimbledon, if you go ahead against Leicester they don't mind throwing extra forwards on to pressurise you.

Fortunately we get off to a good, if contested, start in the 12th minute. Simon Grayson plays a back-pass to his keeper, Kevin Poole, who picks the ball up on the edge of his penalty area. To us, and in particular, the alert Nick Barmby, that's an indirect free-kick. The referee, Jeff Winter, agrees, and while Leicester's players argue, Nick passes the ball quickly to Andy Hinchcliffe, who scores from 20-yards as Poole watches helplessly. But it's his own fault. If he'd kicked the ball away rather than handling it, there would have been no problem.

We are playing with confidence and we aren't really troubled in the first half. Two minutes into stoppage time, Winter books me for time-wasting and even though

Leicester won't be happy with him, I'm not too pleased, either, because since our goal we aren't getting many 50-50 decisions. Winter didn't need to bring out the yellow card just seconds from half-time. All he had to do is tell me to speed things up.

We expect Leicester to come at us after the break but, as in the first half, we score quite early after the kick-off. Ferguson turns back a Hinchcliffe corner and David Unsworth beats Poole from close range. Leicester aren't too demoralised and they push forward, but we show in this game that we have got fight. Unzy's sliding tackle, where he clatters into a referee's assistant, causes great amusement—not least because the poor fella is injured, stretchered off, and has to be replaced!

What is less amusing, however, is Steve Walsh's header which beats me in the 83rd minute. Now Leicester really pile on the pressure and they launch so many high balls into our box that the gaffer takes off Granty and brings on Craig Short as an extra defender. We manage to hold out and record our seventh unbeaten League game. This win now takes us up to sixth place, ahead of Manchester United who drew at Middlesbrough. Better still, after 14 matches we are only six points behind Newcastle, who lead the table. Time to take us seriously again.

Leicester City 1 Everton 2
Southall; Barrett, Watson, Unsworth; Stuart,
Parkinson, Grant (Short 84), Speed,
Hinchcliffe; Ferguson, Barmby.
Subs (not used): Hottiger, Branch, Allen, Gerrard.
Attendance: 20,975

NOVEMBER 28

Everton announce they have made a trading loss of
nearly £8 million last season. Most of this, I understand,
is accounted for by the £5 million we paid for Andrei
Kanchelskis.

NOVEMBER 30

Everton v Sunderland
This is typical Everton. We are on a good run, while
Sunderland are struggling and haven't scored an away
League goal since August. We really mess things up
today. I admit I'm a little concerned about our team. I
think Joe Royle could be making a mistake in dropping
Duncan Ferguson for Andrei, who is fit again. The reason
I'm worried is that Sunderland always play with five
men in midfield, so you cannot play through them. You
can't go round them either, because of the way they pack
the midfield, so the only way to beat them is by going

over them. That's where Duncan comes in. We need to bypass the midfield to serve him. It may not be the prettiest way of trying to win a game, but this is a case of needs must.

Lionel Perez saves a Kanchelskis cross-shot with his legs in the first half, but Sunderland are more dangerous than we are, with my former Everton team-mate, Paul Bracewell, running midfield. I make saves from Kevin Ball and Alex Rae, and just when it seems Gary Speed will head us into the lead, Bracewell clears off the line.

Even though we are struggling, I still think we might get something from their goalkeeper. But Perez, much to my surprise, handles every cross superbly, and he even saves a Graham Stuart penalty early into the second half after Diamond is shoved by Martin Scott.

Fergie replaces Tony Grant, but before he can make an impression Craig Russell opens the scoring in the 54th minute with a header from David Kelly's centre. The game opens up with Perez saving well from Kanchelskis and me having to kick a shot from Russell onto the post. Michael Branch then comes on for Andrei and in the 63rd minute, Fergie proves a point to the gaffer by planting a powerful header in the net from an Andy Hinchcliffe corner.

I fancy our chances of getting the win, but we are all stunned by two late goals from substitute Michael Bridges. This is a good win for Sunderland, but we have made it easy for them by not getting our tactics right. The booing from our fans at the final whistle says it all.

Everton 1 Sunderland 3

Southall; Barrett, Watson, Unsworth,
Hinchcliffe (Short 81); Kanchelskis (Branch 61),
Grant (Ferguson 52), Parkinson, Speed;
Stuart, Barmby.
Subs (not used): Hottiger, Gerrard.

Attendance: 40,087

DECEMBER

		Pts
6	CHELSEA	24
7	ASTON VILLA	24
8	EVERTON	23
9	DERBY COUNTY	21
10	SHEFFIELD WED	21

MONDAY, DECEMBER 2

Jimmy Gabriel announces that he is to leave the club at the end of the season—37 years after he first walked through the door as a player. He intends to continue coaching in America. Jimmy, who is Everton through and through, is our reserve team coach. The young lads have a lot of time for him and it will be a sad loss for the club when he goes.

DECEMBER 5

A story in the Press says the club is considering moving to a new stadium. I don't know anything about this, and I always take things in the Press with a pinch of salt After all we have been linked with a few players recently, but nothing has happened.

DECEMBER 7

Chelsea v Everton

Duncan Ferguson is back in the starting line-up to re-place Nick Barmby, who has 'flu. Chelsea begin with five foreigners in their side, plus another, Roberto Di Matteo, on the bench. They are strange to play against. They allow us space, but they seem to have acquired a nasty streak under Ruud Gullit's management. That's a sign of a good team.

The little Italian, Gianfranco Zola, is having a great game, and he puts Chelsea ahead in the 12th minute with a free-kick which will probably look worse than it is. Earl Barrett is standing at my right post to protect it. It's my decision to put him there. If Zola's shot had been a foot lower, Earl would have blocked it, but it's well-placed and I end up diving and landing on Earl, which must look stupid. In fact, the ball is in the net before I can get over.

We are only behind for five minutes, when Michael Branch scores his first goal for the club. Andy Hinchcliffe sends over a deep cross which Duncan heads on and Branchy flicks the ball over Frode Grodas from six yards. I'm pleased for him because a few of us had started to think he was another Stuart Barlow—a player who would have loads of chances but who couldn't score.

Branchy can become a really good player provided he keeps thinking he's Michael Branch and not anyone else.

He has to be his own man more. At the moment he's copying too many people at the club. It's time he finds out what suits him, not what suits other people. I don't think his problem is a lack of ability. Some of the runs he makes are fantastic; they remind me of the ones Ian Rush makes. Michael is lightning quick, but I don't think our style is helping him. He is getting into the channels but we don't pick him out. All we do is look for Duncan Ferguson. Fergie plays a big part in our second goal in the 28th minute, when he launches a pass over Scott Minto's head for Andrei to sprint clear and score with a confident finish.

Zola's first half is impressive, which annoys me because I had seen him against Leeds recently when Lucas Radebe did a man-marking job on him and he didn't get a kick. It's only in the second half that we decide to put a man on him. Mind you, it still doesn't stop him crossing for Gianluca Vialli to head home in the 55th minute.

Chelsea start to pressurise us further and we survive a few dangerous moments. I'm happy with a point. It's just frustrating to see that Sunderland, who beat us 3-1 at home last weekend, have gone down at their place by the same score to Wimbledon, who have amazingly moved into second place, four points behind leaders Arsenal, but with a game in hand.

Chelsea 2 Everton 2

Southall; Barrett, Watson, Unsworth, Hinchcliffe;
Kanchelskis, Parkinson, Grant, Speed;
Ferguson, Branch (Stuart 71).
Subs (not used): Rideout, Hottiger, Short, Gerrard.

Attendance: 28,418

DECEMBER 11

Vinny Samways finally gets his wish and leaves Everton.
He signs for Las Palmas in the Spanish Second Division
for £700,000.

DECEMBER 14

Wales v Turkey

Bobby Gould changes his tactics here, giving Watford's
Robbie Page a debut in defence and using Gary Speed as
sweeper. The Turks are no mugs. They hit the bar and
then I make a save from Kemalettin, before their keeper,
Engin, pushes a Mark Hughes shot for a corner.

We don't do too badly, but we lose our way midway
through the second half, when Turkey step up a gear. I
parry a shot from Hakan Sukur and the same player
forces me to block another shot. I'm grateful this time
that Robbie Page clears off the line. We needed to win
this one.

Wales 0 Turkey 0
Southall; Jenkins, Page, V. Jones, Melville,
Pembridge, Horne, Speed, Saunders (Hartson 83),
M. Hughes, Giggs.
Attendance: 14,206

DECEMBER 16

Derby County v Everton
This isn't a great pitch and it's not a great game—another
one on a Monday night—but I'm not bothered because
we pick up an important win. Derby have the better
chances, even though our line-up is very attack-minded.

We give the ball away far too much in the first 20
minutes and I'm a bit worried. I save Ashley Ward's
volley and Aljosa Asanovic misses two good chances,
the first he blasts over the bar and the second he heads
over. We shouldn't be allowing sides opportunities like
that.

We think we should have a penalty when Paul McGrath
wrestles Nick Barmby to the ground, but the referee,
Mike Reed, doesn't want to know.

Joe Parkinson dominates midfield and is without doubt
our man-of-the-match. With four minutes left he smashes
a shot against the crossbar and Nick is the quickest to
react as he knocks the rebound in . . . with his nose!

This is a fairly steady Everton performance, but Sky
are touting us as potential champions. I definitely don't

think we are rubbish, but I would love to see us sign someone who could score 20 goals a season to play alongside Duncan. I know that's easier said than done, but our squad is still thin.

Having said that, we are all fairly optimistic about putting another good run together. We are back up to seventh and we have four home games coming up. What's more, our next one away is against Middlesbrough, who haven't won in the League since they beat us at Goodison in September. A healthy collection of points from these fixtures would certainly worry a few people.

Derby County 0 Everton 1
Southall; Barrett, Watson, Unsworth, Hinchcliffe; Kanchelskis, Parkinson, Barmby, Speed; Branch (Stuart 46), Ferguson.
Subs (not used): Rideout, Hottiger, Short, Gerrard.
Attendance: 17,252

DECEMBER 21

Everton v Leeds United
An awful game, but one in which my opposite number Nigel Martyn and I both have work to do. David Unsworth, who will be banned for two games in the New Year, is on the bench today as Craig Short is brought back into defence. We need to improve on our inconsistent

home form, and the fact that a win would take us into fourth place should be our motivation.

But we don't play well. Lee Sharpe forces me to beat out his shot when he is inside the area, while at the other end, Martyn gets down well to save from Gary Speed. Gary seems desperate to score against his old club and I would love him to do so.

However, we enjoy two more escapes in the first half. Firstly I turn a David Wetherall effort round the post and then, as we fail to clear the corner, Ian Rush mistimes a header from six yards. I've been so used to Rushie putting that kind of chance away over the years that I'm mightily relieved this time. We finish the half well, but Andrei, having brought a parry out of Martyn, hits the rebound over the top of an empty goal. I can't believe it.

Leeds are still dangerous in the second half. Rushie puts Brian Deane away and he only has me to beat, but thankfully he shoots over. Our defence is getting caught square too often and I have to turn a drive from Deane for a corner.

There is nothing I can do on the hour when Gary Kelly curls a shot onto our crossbar. But that is nothing like the let-off we have two minutes from time when Deane is on the goal-line and still can't score. Don't ask me how he can't stick that one in. I bet he doesn't know, either. I think we've just seen the miss of the season.

Our gaffer says afterwards how well Nigel Martyn has played, which is really nice and just what I want to hear!

But just as disappointing as the result for us is the injury to Andy Hinchcliffe, as a result of an awkward first half fall. To be fair to our physio, Les Helm, he doesn't get a good view of the fall and he is unsure of the damage to Andy. He allows him to carry on playing but he is clearly not right and is replaced by Michael Branch in the 61st minute. The damage appears to have been done to a cruciate ligament. Word is he won't play again this season. That's a huge blow to us in view of the number of goals he makes. Unless the gaffer is thinking of playing Unzy down the left, I think he'll have to go and buy a replacement for Andy. The next few days should be interesting. I still wish Joe Royle would sign a striker, though, because we just aren't getting enough goals. And our style of play is too predictable.

Also on this day, the club is given permission to build a new School of Excellence in the Netherton area of the city. Ideally this sounds great, and I hope work begins quickly. I've trained on this land and it's a good site for a place to house and train the YTS lads. But it's important that it's run properly. If it is, then we could become the leader in this field in the Premier League.

Everton 0 Leeds United 0
Southall; Barrett, Watson, Short (Unsworth 42), Hinchcliffe (Branch 61); Kanchelskis, Parkinson, Grant, Speed; Barmby, Ferguson.
Subs (not used): Rideout, Stuart, Gerrard.
Attendance: 36,954

DECEMBER 23

Matt Jackson, who has spent weeks on loan at Birmingham, joins Norwich City for £450,000. Matt is an easy-going lad and I think this move will suit him down to the ground. He is a better player than he thinks. He just lacks self-belief. If he realises the ability he has he could still become a great player.

Matt needs to get away from Everton because it's obvious he's not going to play here. I don't think Birmingham would have been right for him because there is too much turmoil there, even though he knows Gary Ablett and Barry Horne. Norwich are more settled and Mike Walker knows what he can do, having managed him at Everton.

I'll miss Matt because he's such a good lad to have around.

DECEMBER 26

Middlesbrough v Everton
It's not just our morale which is bruised after this defeat. We were already without the injured Craig Short and Andy Hinchcliffe, plus Andrei Kanchelskis who is ill, but after only 14 minutes we lose Dave Watson with damaged ribs. Young Graham Allen replaces him. What kind of team will we be able to put out against Wimbledon the

day after tomorrow? I wonder if we should do what Middlesbrough have done and tell the FA we aren't playing because we can't raise a side. . . .

Middlesbrough don't appear like a club with an injury crisis to me. I don't care who they may or may not have missing because they won't miss anyone as much as we will miss Waggy. We begin brightly, however, as Nick Barmby—not surprisingly booed by the home crowd—sends over a corner which Speedo smacks against a post. We think we should have a penalty soon afterwards when Nick is clattered to the ground in the box, but referee Steven Dunn waves play on.

'Boro give us a warning through a Fabrizio Ravanelli header which Diamond nods off the line. But we don't heed it as Craig Hignett slots Emerson's pass past me for the opening goal. We draw level from a David Unsworth penalty, which is awarded for a needless handball by Derek Whyte.

Clayton Blackmore's 20-yard curler restores Middlesbrough's lead, only for Fergie to beat Gary Walsh with a firm header to equalise again. However, we are poor in the second half. Juninho suddenly takes control, scoring their third goal after I block a shot. We really let things slip when Marc Hottiger is brought on for Allen as we try to push forward. In doing so, we are a mess at the back. We defend far too deeply, letting Middlesbrough run with the ball. With Juninho around this is fatal, and he scores another.

This result again highlights the importance of Waggy to Everton and also our lack of consistency. I have experienced better Christmases.

Middlesbrough 4 Everton 2
Southall; Barrett, Watson (Allen 14 (Hottiger 71)),
Unsworth; Stuart, Grant, Parkinson, Barmby, Speed;
Ferguson, Branch (Rideout 66).
Subs (not used): Limpar, Gerrard.
Attendance: 29,673

DECEMBER 28

Everton v Wimbledon
When you have just let four goals in the last team you want to face are Wimbledon—particularly as we are without Andy Hinchcliffe, of course, but also Dave Watson, Andrei Kanchelskis, Joe Parkinson and Craig Short.

Joe Royle brings back Ebbo, who has missed 10 games with a hairline fracture of the ankle, and he gives Paul Rideout and Marc Hottiger their first starts since that awful game at York. So stretched are we that another teenager, full-back John Hills, is one of the substitutes. I am named captain in Dave's absence.

Wimbledon lost their previous game 5-0 at Aston Villa, but had their Boxing Day fixture postponed. They are obviously fresher than we are, but we don't do badly in the first half and go ahead in the 23rd minute. Ebbo plays a marvellous pass which splits Wimbledon's defence, and Graham Stuart coolly sweeps the ball past Neil Sullivan. Duncan wastes a great chance to put us two up by directing a free header straight at Sullivan from Nick Barmby's centre.

Two brilliant challenges within seconds by Earl Barrett on Efan Ekoku warn us not to rest on our laurels, and Wimbledon are even more dangerous after the break. I save an Oyvind Leonhardsen drive which deflects off Vinny Jones, and then I touch a shot from Neil Ardley around the post. Unfortunately, Ardley's corner skims off David Unsworth's head and Ekoku loops a header over me and into the net.

Dean Blackwell's goal-line header from Stuart prevents our regaining the lead with a superb 40-yard attempt, but we fall behind to a Leonhardsen shot in the 69th minute. Six minutes later, as we push forward in search of an equaliser, Ekoku feeds Marcus Gayle, who rounds me and scores Wimbledon's third.

Hills, who cost £60,000 from Blackpool, gets his first taste of first team football when he replaces Ebbo in the 80th minute. He has made good progress in the reserves and he's another one for the future. It's a pity the present isn't looking good—and that our home form is terrible.

Everton 1 Wimbledon 3
Southall; Hottiger, Barrett, Unsworth, Speed;
Stuart, Ebbrell (Hills 80), Grant, Barmby;
Ferguson, Rideout (Branch 73).
Subs (not used): Allen, Limpar, Gerrard.
Attendance: 36,733

DECEMBER 30

Joe Royle pays Chelsea £850,000 for Terry Phelan. We've
needed a left-sided player to replace Andy Hinchcliffe,
but I'm not sure he is the right choice. Whenever I've
seen Terry's name it's been alongside hamstring or thigh
strain. He's a very quick player, but the quicker you are,
the more you tend to injure your hamstrings and thighs.
We don't need any more injuries!

Maybe I'm being a bit harsh. He might turn out to be
a good buy because he's a full international, and to get
one for under £1 million is good business. Terry is obviously a good player. I'm just concerned about how many
games he'll be able to play for us.

JANUARY

		Pts
6	ASTON VILLA	34
7	CHELSEA	32
8	EVERTON	28
9	SHEFFIELD WED	28
10	TOTTENHAM H	28

WEDNESDAY, JANUARY 1

Everton v Blackburn Rovers
Another bad game which makes the festive period even worse for us. We could hardly have got the New Year off to a worse start. We are absolutely awful, hardly creating a chance, and Blackburn are worthy winners. This result takes them out of the bottom three. It is really getting to me that we continue to slip up against the lesser sides. I'm also annoyed by our home form, which is becoming abysmal.

The fact that Andrei is playing while still suffering the effects of 'flu is no excuse. Nor is the fact that Waggy and Ebbo have had pain-killing jabs and that we have players injured and suspended, which explains the presence of yet another teenager—Richard Dunne—on the bench. We play without spirit and without passion in this match. We are rubbish.

Tim Sherwood gives Blackburn the lead in the 17th

minute, running onto Chris Sutton's pass to shoot past me. Fifteen minutes later it's all over for us as Sherwood slides a pass to Kevin Gallacher. He finds Sutton who produces another good finish.

Blackburn are well on top. We are fortunate that they are not as composed in their finishing as on previous occasions. Joe Royle takes off Nick Barmby at half-time and throws on Michael Branch. Nick has hardly been in the game and the doubts about which is his best position are being raised again. The only time we look like scoring is late in the second half, but Tim Flowers saves well from Gary Speed. Again, we are too predictable. We still rely on the high ball to Duncan. We need an alternative to that.

The League table shows we are now 10 points off third from top and 10 points off third from bottom. We have become a mid-table team and we don't look as if we are going anywhere. We are starting to feel the pressure a bit and our confidence is down.

We are fortunate to have a home FA Cup tie against Swindon coming up to take our minds off the League. But we know that if we go out against them we are going to come in for some right stick.

Everton 0 Blackburn Rovers 2

Southall; Hottiger, Watson, Barrett, Phelan;
Kanchelskis (Limpar 70), Ebbrell, Stuart,
Speed; Ferguson, Barmby (Branch 46).
Subs (not used): Rideout, Dunne, Gerrard.

Attendance: 30,427

JANUARY 5

Everton v Swindon Town
(FA Cup 3rd Round)

This is an eventful game which begins with another
piece of Everton history when Richard Dunne becomes
the club's youngest player to appear in a first team match
at Goodison. He's just 17, but you wouldn't think so to
look at him. At 6' 2" and over 15 stone, he's a big lad. And
he isn't at all fazed by the fact that he's making his debut.

Dunny is the first product from our alliance with the
Irish club Home Farm Everton. I rate him. In fact, he
could go on to become another Paul McGrath. He's got
pace, composure and he uses both feet. That's all he
needs. I just hope that as he gets older he's able to control
his weight. Richard is a quiet boy with a good attitude,
although he does like his bed! I think we have a good
player here.

To many people, Swindon, managed by Steve
McMahon, are perfectly equipped to cause an upset,
especially as we haven't been playing well. But I know

we'll get through this tie. We are helped, it's true, by the sending off of Ian Culverhouse after just . . . 52 seconds! His offence is to handle Andrei's shot in the area, even though Swindon seem to be saying the ball hit his chest. Andrei isn't complaining, of course, and his penalty gives us just the calming start we need.

You know that a team which is managed by McMahon will play decent football but will also show some steel. That is Swindon, but with Paul Rideout amazing us all by playing in midfield and doing superbly there, we are in charge. Ridders even manages to head against the crossbar. He is a much better player than a lot of people give him credit for. I think he should play more often because he is showing us he can be a useful midfielder as well as a good striker. We already know he can be a centre-half as well, and when he's up front, he holds the ball up better than Fergie. In a team like ours it's so important for the forwards to hold the ball and bring people into play. With Paul being the best at the club at doing this, I don't know why we haven't made more use of him. He is almost as good at holding the ball up as Mark Hughes—and that's saying something.

That's not to say we aren't given any scares. Kevin Horlock's powerful header forces me into a save, but I'm beaten by an excellent Mark Walters chip which, thankfully, hits the bar. Walters is even more unfortunate when his suicidal back-pass is intercepted by Nick Barmby, who rounds Fraser Digby to score our second goal.

Early into the second half Duncan increases our lead with a brilliant header from Earl Barrett's cross. We should score even more goals, not least when Gary Elkins is sent off 16 minutes from time for showing too much of that steel. I'm not sure he deserved to go off. Okay, it's not the first crude foul he's made, but this is a Cup tie after all and players are going to be committed. Or, at least, they should be. Sadly these days if you sneeze you get a yellow card and if you sneeze twice you get a red one.

Everton 3 Swindon Town 0
Southall; Barrett, Watson, Dunne;
Kanchelskis; Stuart, Rideout, Speed;
Barmby, Branch, Ferguson (Grant 85).
Subs (not used): Hottiger, Gerrard.
Attendance: 20,411

JANUARY 11

Sheffield Wednesday v Everton
This is one of my busiest games of the season, especially in the first hour when Wednesday pummel us. I like to think that even though we are under the cosh, my work has still given us a chance of obtaining at least a point.

Unzy is available after suspension, but Richard Dunne keeps his place following his impressive performance against Swindon. However, none of our three central

midfielders—Joe Parkinson, John Ebbrell and Tony Grant—
are in the starting line-up, so the defensive duties there
fall to Ridders and Diamond. Good though these lads
are, defending is not their game, and we really struggle
as Wednesday run through us at will.

I save a Mark Pembridge drive and a Ritchie Humphreys
cross-shot, but our defending is very poor—highlighted
by the way my defensive wall leaps in unison when
facing Pembridge's 21st minute free-kick. As a result, the
ball clips the heel of one of my team-mates and deflects
past me. I'm furious at this lack of cover. The only time
Wednesday are threatened in what is an abysmal first
half for us is when one of their own players, Guy
Whittingham, strangely fires at his own goal, forcing
Kevin Pressman into a great save.

Dunny is doing well enough, but he loses concentra-
tion early in the second half, allowing David Hirst to beat
him in the air on the halfway line. Hirst's pass sends
Humphreys away and Hirst supports him to convert
with a tap-in.

It's only when we send on Granty that we look dangerous. Duncan plants a header against the Wednesday
bar, but he pulls a goal back from a cross from another
substitute, Michael Branch—and he suddenly enjoys a
purple patch. Pressman, who is outstanding, pulls off a
great save to touch Duncan's shot from a corner, and
then he does even better to stop a Gary Speed header.

I have to make a save from Hirst before we apply more

pressure, with Fergie heading against the outside of a post. But we pay the price for our wretched 60 minutes. It's so hard when you have to chase a game, and it's more evident than ever that we still need to strengthen our squad.

Sheffield Wednesday 2 Everton 1

Southall; Barrett, Watson, Dunne (Unsworth 62), Phelan (Branch 46); Kanchelskis, Rideout (Grant 50), Stuart, Speed; Barmby; Ferguson.
Subs (not used): Limpar, Gerrard.

Attendance: 24,175

JANUARY 15

Joe Royle enters the transfer market, paying Ipswich Town £900,000 for Claus Thomsen. We have tended to play one good half and one bad one, and if he can help us find more consistency then both he and the gaffer will have done well.

To be honest, I don't know Claus from my next-door neighbour. He may be a Danish international, but this season I haven't seen or heard his name anywhere. I think that's because he hasn't played many games because of injury. I've even been to watch Denmark play Turkey in my capacity as Wales coach, mainly to check on the Turks, who we were going to meet, but I didn't know Claus was playing in that match!

You can't grumble when your club signs an international, though because I don't know anything about him I'm not sure if he's the right man. But you shouldn't judge anyone until they have played a few games. I've heard he can play in defence or in midfield, so it will be interesting to see what he can do.

JANUARY 16

Everton arrange a game against German side Arminia Bielefeld for February 7 in . . . China. It will be a good experience and all that, but I don't see the point of playing so far away.

JANUARY 18

Anders Limpar is sold to Birmingham on a six-month deal for £100,000. I'm surprised it's taken him this long to go. I've lost count of the number of times he's said he is fed up. His face is so long he's in danger of tripping up on it one day. You can't have unhappy players at a club, so it's best he leaves. Anders has loads of ability, and in training he does some fantastic things, but he is inconsistent on the playing field. He's been accused of having no heart, but I think he has tried in his own way. When things are going his way, he is brilliant. When they're not, then you don't need him around because he won't do anything defensively.

The situation we are in now requires people who will tackle and be prepared to get hurt. I reckon we need 10 Dave Watsons to help us stabilise. Anders is not that type of player. If we were playing good football, then I'm sure we'd have seen more of him—but we're not. If we don't buck our ideas up, we're going to find ourselves in the relegation zone.

JANUARY 19

Arsenal v Everton
Arsenal don't beat us today, they annihilate us. We don't start off too badly, though. Unzy is back, while Claus Thomsen makes a steady debut in midfield. I save twice from Paul Merson, who is looking dangerous, but we think we have taken the lead in the 29th minute when Nick Barmby hooks superbly past David Seaman. Keith Burge, the referee, rules the effort out for offside. I can't see if he's right from where I am, but looking at the other lads I think he's made a mistake.

Seaman then dives to his right to parry from Duncan, and when Ian Wright doesn't appear for the second half we reckon we have a chance of getting something out of this game. But things start to go horribly wrong just nine minutes after the re-start when Wright's replacement,

Lee Dixon, lobs a ball into our box and Dennis Bergkamp reacts quickest to stroke it home.

Two minutes later, we fail to clear a corner and Patrick Vieira crashes a left foot shot through a crowd of defenders and past me for Arsenal's second goal. Bergkamp looks set to score again almost immediately, but I manage to stop him. I block again from Bergkamp in the 68th minute as he intercepts Unsworth's pass, but this time the rebound falls kindly for Merson, who scores unchallenged.

Even though we can point to Nick's disallowed goal as an excuse, I really don't think it would have altered this result, because Arsenal are rampant in the second half. It might have been worse for us if Wright hadn't been injured. Fergie pulls a goal back for us with a soaring header one minute from time, which suggests that things could have been different if we had got more crosses in. But it's a case of too little too late.

We have now got ourselves into the habit of losing, which is dangerous. We have also kept only two clean sheets in our last 13 Premiership fixtures. This is not good for morale, but it's at times like this that a positive attitude is needed. It's so easy to start feeling sorry for ourselves. If we do that, then things are hardly going to improve. Perhaps another win in the Cup will give us the lift we want.

Arsenal 3 Everton 1

Southall; Barrett, Unsworth, Watson, Phelan;
Kanchelskis (Branch 62), Thomsen, Stuart,
Speed; Barmby, Ferguson.
Subs (not used): Rideout, Grant, Short, Gerrard.

Attendance: 38,095

JANUARY 25

Everton v Bradford City
(FA Cup 4th Round)

Sickening. Absolutely sickening. On paper this is a good
tie for us because even though our home record is poor,
Bradford are a division below us—and fighting to stay
there. Having said that, what have they to lose today?
Nothing at all. This is their FA Cup final and they are
going to make the most of it.

Shorty is back for Unzy, but we are feeling the
pressure of recent results and it shows early on when
Chris Waddle plays John Dreyer in, who wastes the opportunity. Waddle is looking lively—he's certainly carrying
Bradford's hopes. He gives us another warning on the
half hour when he smashes a free-kick against the frame
of my goal. Strangely, I'm feeling less comfortable about
this game than I was about the one against Swindon.

It's not as if Bradford dominate. They are dangerous
going forward, but at the back they look unsteady. Their
keeper, Mark Schwarzer, blocks from Nick Barmby in the

first half and then he makes an even better save from Duncan Ferguson.

But we ruin things after the break. Waddle finds Dreyer again in the 49th minute, but this time the defender hooks a good shot into the roof of my net. Our supporters are anxious, and they become angry a minute later when Andrei Kanchelskis dithers on the ball just inside our half. I'm quite advanced because I'm expecting him to pass the ball back. I don't know what the hell he is doing, but he loses possession and Waddle scores with a brilliant 40-yard lob.

Joe Royle has come in for a lot of criticism from the media and from some of our fans. He reckons there has been a vendetta against him by the local Press. If we lose this game, a lot of people outside the club will be demanding his head.

We are grateful for a quick reply in the 53rd minute, thanks to an own goal from Bradford's young centre-back, Andrew O'Brien. But we find ourselves two goals behind again soon afterwards as Waddle, who is at the heart of everything, finds Swedish striker Robert Steiner, who finishes clinically. Steiner is having a good game, and on this form I can't imagine how Bradford are so low in their division.

Fergie misses a great chance to get us back into the game when he miss-kicks just past the hour, and he chooses to pass to Nick Barmby later on when everyone expects him to attempt a header at goal.

I'll have that: I save from Alan Shearer—and try to steal his boot!
—17 August 1996

A friendly chat with referee Graham Poll
—21 August 1996

The flying Welshman: my save from Manchester United's Ryan Giggs
—21 August 1996

Ooh! Ah! … Speedo and Eric Cantona in action
—21 August 1996

above:
Ain't no mountain high enough: Andrei Kanchelskis leaps over Villa's Steve Staunton —4 September 1996

left:
Paul Gerrard— my Everton rival

The one that got away: I can only watch as Middlesbrough score at Goodison
—14 September 1996

Middlesbrough's Fabrizio Ravanelli is up for it—but I get there first
—14 September 1996

above:
Graham Stuart congratulates
Craig Short on his goal at
Nottingham Forest.
Left to right: David Unsworth,
Michael Branch, Shorty,
Diamond, Earl Barrett and
Gary Speed
—28 October 1996

right:
Fergie leaps into action—
then gets sent off!
—21 September 1996

"…and no mustard": just ordering a snack!
—21 September 1996

Ridders puts us ahead against York City
—24 September 1996

Holding their own: Everton's wall prepare to block a free kick

The lads celebrate Andrei's first-minute goal as the Swindon players walk away dejected—5 January 1997

Spurs goalkeeper Ian Walker saves at Waggy's feet
—12 April 1997

above:
Handbags at dawn!
John Barnes and
Michael Thomas act as
referees to separate Unzy
and Robbie Fowler
—16 April 1997

right:
Paul Rideout, heading East

Everton 1996-97—*Back row (left to right)*: John Ebbrell, Tony Grant, Vinny Samways, Paul Gerrard, Neville Southall, Andy Hinchcliffe, Matt Jackson, Joe Parkinson. *Middle row (left to right)*: Jimmy Martin (kit manager), Jimmy Gabriel (reserve team coach), Craig Short, Earl Barrett, Graham Allen, Jon O'Connor, Willie Donachie (assistant manager), Les Helm. *Front row (left to right)*: Graham Stuart, Michael Branch, Gary Speed, Andrei Kanchelskis, Joe Royle (manager), Dave Watson (captain), Marc Hottiger, Duncan Ferguson, David Unsworth.

We can't throw on an extra striker—such as Michael Branch—because the manager hasn't named a forward among his three substitutes, which seems strange. Still, we pull another goal back in the last minute when Gary Speed's left-wing cross deceives Schwarzer and ends up in the net. As at Arsenal, it comes too late to save us, and the crowd don't hesitate in booing us off at the end. Some of them even direct their anger at Duncan, which I have never seen before. I always thought he was a god to Evertonians.

Having said that, I can understand the fans' reaction. Everton supporters love the Cup. They have great affection for this trophy and they seem to want to win it more than the Championship because of the glory that goes with it.

In the dressing room, Andrei apologises for his mistake, but it's too late now. I'm not going to have a go at him because I don't see the point. I've made mistakes over the years, so it wouldn't be right for me to go shouting the odds at him. Mind you, looking at Andrei's face, I think it's the beginning of the end for him. I'm not sure he wants to carry on playing for us. I think he's just about had enough.

I go on a Radio City phone-in after the game and the least I can say is that the verdict on this defeat from the supporters is some way less than positive. A lot of them want Royle out. But I defend him, just as I have already done in the pink edition of the *Liverpool Echo*, where I write a weekly column. We may not be the best team in the world but I still believe Joe is the man we need, even though he doesn't communicate with some of us very well or very often. The only criticism I have against him is that he should have spent more money. The pressure on him must be immense, but he's trying not to show it. As a team, we have now reached the stage where we are under less pressure when we play away from home, and that can't be right.

Everton 2 Bradford City 3
Southall; Barrett, Watson, Short, Phelan (Grant 57); Kanchelskis, Parkinson, Stuart, Speed; Ferguson, Barmby.
Subs (not used): Unsworth, Gerrard.
Attendance: 30,007

JANUARY 27

This is one of the worst days of my career. Joe Royle says he wants a word with me during training. I've no idea what it is about, and I am stunned when he tells me he is leaving me out of the game against Newcastle on Wednesday. I ask him why. He replies: "Because I am!"

What kind of a reason is that? He tells me: "You've done nothing wrong, but I think it's time to bring Paul Gerrard in because he's trained well."

Call me naive if you want, but I always thought it was

ability that got you in the team, not because you happen to train well. "Give me a reason!" I say to Royle, and he replies again: "This is the reason: because I am. The time is right."

I am upset by this. Not only am I baffled by this man's lack of logic, I don't feel I deserve to be left out. I know I have often felt uneasy about him, but I have still been one of his biggest public defenders in my column in the *Liverpool Echo*. This is my reward!

There is no doubt Royle is making me the scapegoat for the result against Bradford and, in particular, Chris Waddle's goal. I've said before that I am harsh when it comes to self-criticism, but when I analyse that game again I don't think I played any worse than anyone else in our team. I honestly don't see Royle's reason—not that he's given me a proper one. I feel a great sense of injustice, disbelief and a great deal of anger. People will probably expect me to have a moan against Royle, but I'm not going to kick-off. He's made his decision and nothing I say will make him change it.

I feel the manager should have broken the news to me in private. Taking me to one side on the training pitch, when everyone else can see, is not the best way to do this sort of thing. He has not handled this well.

JANUARY 28

I still haven't got over yesterday's shock. But I am angered even more when I read that the news of my being dropped has made the papers. How the hell did they get hold of it? Royle had told me yesterday not to tell anyone, which I respected. Now I find that someone obviously has.

There are two ways I can react to yesterday's bombshell: I can either go round moping or train as hard as I can. I'm going to do the latter—and I'm going to help Paul Gerrard as much as I can. I've got nothing against him at all. It's not Paul who has dropped me and it's not his fault I'm not playing tomorrow.

I intend treating tomorrow's match as I would any other, despite knowing I'm on the bench. I even play Trivial Pursuit with the boss on the bus up to the North East. I think he feels a bit embarrassed. I'm not—I'm just very, very angry.

The lads—including Paul—are all shocked that I've been dropped. Genuinely shocked. I can tell when they think someone is not good enough to play, and this is not one of those occasions.

JANUARY 29

Newcastle United v Everton

We don't have Andrei Kanchelskis in our side because we are told he is injured. But we learn he has been discussing a move to Fiorentina—a move the media have been speculating about for some time. I'm sure he will go because he's not really been happy this season. Hopefully the money we get for him will be put to good use.

Our starting line-up at Newcastle doesn't include Nick Barmby either, because, after dropping me, Joe Royle also decides our record signing also deserves to lose his place. It goes without saying that Nick isn't thrilled, either. It's a really happy ship!

In the dressing room, I try not to show my disappointment. I try to liven things up, but it's hard. Paul Gerrard seems a little embarrassed about my situation, but he's naturally excited about playing his first full game for Everton at a place like St. James' Park, and good luck to him. Paul and I get on well. We have a good relationship. Yes, we are rivals, but we try to help each other. I'll be watching him carefully because I've not really seen him play. When he came on against Southampton he only had one cross to deal with. If there's any advice I can give him during or after the game, then I will. I know he will appreciate it.

We don't begin this fixture like a team low on morale because we dominate the first half—and beyond. We play some excellent football, giving Newcastle no time or space in which to manoeuvre. Duncan Ferguson misses a good early chance, but Gary Speed cracks home an excellent second minute free-kick which stuns their crowd. We are playing so well that even after we lose Craig Short with concussion before the half hour, I think we can get something from this match.

We waste other opportunities, particularly one where Fergie shoots at Shaka Hislop after he is sent clear. Watching from the sidelines, I'm a bit disappointed with the lack of movement up front. But it's only when Faustino Asprilla comes on for Peter Beardsley in the 57th minute that my optimism starts to wane.

Les Ferdinand hooks in a 73rd minute goal for Newcastle. Six minutes later Robert Lee puts them ahead and suddenly Newcastle are buzzing. Royle sends on Paul Rideout with nine minutes left, but that gives him no time to do anything. Besides, we sense Newcastle have not finished yet. We are right, because when Claus Thomsen fouls the speedy Asprilla, Alan Shearer scores from the spot. Then, two minutes into stoppage time, Robbie Elliott hits Newcastle's fourth. How have we managed to lose so heavily after dominating for so long?

Paul Gerrard can't be blamed for any of the goals. I take no pleasure, by the way, in seeing them fly into our net, even though I wish it was me out there. The fact is we lost. I don't like Everton to lose, whether I'm playing or not.

This is our sixth successive League defeat. It's the last thing we need, but once again it tells us we just aren't good enough. Looking at the League table, we are still in that middle section. But we are only two points off a relegation place, and all the teams in the bottom three have at least one game in hand on us. If we sell Andrei, we have *got* to use that money to buy decent players.

While I am concerned by Everton's future, I have to say I am more concerned about my own. I no longer know what it holds at this club. I think long and hard after the game about where I go from here because it's quite clear that Royle doesn't want me. To be honest, I've felt that ever since he told me to go and sign for Wolves pre-season.

I reckon I have played my last game for Everton. I can't see any way of getting back into the side.

Newcastle United 4 Everton 1
Gerrard; Barrett, Short (Grant 27 (Rideout 81)),
Watson, Unsworth, Phelan; Thomsen,
Parkinson, Speed; Stuart; Ferguson.
Subs (not used): Barmby, Allen, Southall.
Attendance: 36,143

JANUARY 30

As expected, Andrei completes his move to Fiorentina. Everton say the transfer fee is £8 million. If that's right, then good player that he is, I think we have done good business because Andrei's form has been nowhere near as good as last season's. Even with today's inflated prices, you can buy quality players for £8 million. Let's hope we do.

The fans are sympathetic to me. True, I've already had a couple of letters saying that I was good once and now it's time I moved over. But most of the correspondence is very positive and encouraging. I've had to laugh, though, at a couple of letters which slag me off and end with something like: "Can you send my lad an autograph because he thinks you're great?"

I'm pleased the supporters are with me. It's nice to know I've not been fooling myself when I've thought I've played well. I don't know what Joe Royle's problem is with me. He knows I have ambitions to become a manager, but I honestly don't think he sees me as a threat to his job here. I've been at this club for a long time—perhaps he finds that difficult to cope with. He has told the Press after yesterday's game that the deciding factor in choosing Paul Gerrard ahead of me was Paul's ability on crosses. But really, I wonder if he thought: "I'll shake everybody up by dropping Neville Southall because he has played well." In other words, he'd be giving out the message that nobody is safe. That's a bit daft, I know, but if that had been his reason, then I would have accepted it more easily than the explanation I have been given.

Whatever his thoughts, I don't see the point of dropping somebody who has been doing well. Surely that weakens your team. And, God knows, we are weak enough already. I'll say this, too: there are people in the Everton side who have not played as well as I have, but they haven't been dropped. That's obvious to everyone. The whole business is very strange. Maybe Royle is feeling the pressure too much. Maybe he feels he has to do something to ease the pressure on him and that affects his thinking.

Royle may not rate me any more, but at least Bobby Gould does. He comes out and backs me publicly, which I really appreciate. Bobby says to the Press that I will still be his number one for Wales, even if I don't play another club game before the end of the season.

We have a friendly against the Republic of Ireland coming up next month, but I've withdrawn from the squad to give Nottingham Forest's Mark Crossley a chance.

JANUARY 31

John Hills joins Swansea City on a month's loan. This is good experience for him and should help him develop further as a professional, not least because he will be working with a good manager, Jan Molby, and playing in a side which has promotion ambitions.

FEBRUARY

		Pts
10	LEEDS UTD	29
11	SUNDERLAND	29
12	EVERTON	28
13	LEICESTER CITY	27
14	COVENTRY CITY	26

SATURDAY, FEBRUARY 1

Everton v Nottingham Forest
We've heard that our proposed trip to China is off. I'm far from heartbroken at this news because in view of our League position, we need to concentrate fully on the important matches. Today's against Forest is vital. Defeat would not only mean we have lost seven League games on the trot—something Everton have *never* done before—it would also put us in the relegation mire, despite our position in the table suggesting otherwise.

Nick Barmby is back in our team, but Craig Short's head injury still rules him out. The fans are right behind us from the start, obviously responding to Joe Royle's plea for vocal backing. If we lose this game, we won't be able to fault them. They at the foot of the table, more desperate for points than we are, but what a sorry, diabolical lot they look.

I thought that, with Stuart Pearce in charge and with

just one defeat in six matches, Forest would at least put up a fight. We are in total control, Graham Stuart forcing Mark Crossley to save with his legs and then making him parry away another shot.

The only time Paul Gerrard is bothered in a one-sided first half is when he goes down to stop Pearce's deflected free-kick. Despite our pressure, I'd be a lot more confident if we take a lead into half-time. We almost get it when a cross by Terry Phelan, who is playing really well, is headed to Earl Barrett by Claus Thomsen. But Crossley turns Earl's effort against a post.

Fortunately, the second half is only two minutes old when Duncan Ferguson skilfully controls Diamond's flick, to take the ball around Steve Chettle and Crossley and open the scoring. We increase our pressure with Claus' shot being cleared off the line by Colin Cooper. Then Nick sends Diamond away, only for Pearce to make a brilliant saving tackle.

Crossley turns Gary Speed's drive for a corner in the 64th minute. The ball falls to David Unsworth, who sends it back across goal, where Duncan heads against a post and Nick converts the rebound. Diamond misses a chance to grab our third goal, but it doesn't matter. We have done more than enough to win this game, and the standing ovation from our supporters at the end proves it.

This is one of our easiest matches of the season, and I can't help thinking that Forest have had it. They are not in the bottom three, but if they continue to be this spineless then they sure as hell will be. As for ourselves, we should gain a lot of confidence from this.

Everton 2 Nottingham Forest 0

Gerrard; Barrett, Watson, Unsworth, Phelan; Parkinson, Thomsen, Speed; Barmby; Stuart, Ferguson.
Subs (not used): Hottiger, Allen, Rideout, Dunne, Southall.
Attendance: 32,567

FEBRUARY 11

Wales draw 0-0 with the Republic of Ireland and my replacement, Mark Crossley, plays a blinder. I'm pleased for him, but it means extra competition for me.

FEBRUARY 13

I need to play a game. It's been nearly three weeks since my last one, which is why I'm turning out for our reserve side against Sheffield Wednesday at Southport's Haig Avenue ground, which is where our reserves play. Jimmy Gabriel has told me I'll be playing.

I don't know where Haig Avenue is—I've never even been to Southport—and I have to get directions from David Prentice, who reports on Everton for the *Liverpool*

Echo. But I give myself two hours to get there from my home in Llandudno, and I arrive a quarter of an hour later than our reporting time. That shocks a few people, I think. Not because I'm late but because I've bothered to turn up at all!

I have missed playing, so I enjoy the game. David Hirst and Ritchie Humphreys play for Wednesday and we draw 1-1. The lights are a problem, though, and I can't always see the ball properly. But I'm glad I'm here—I want to prove to Joe Royle that I am a good professional. I can't afford to muck about because it would tarnish my reputation. Everton pay my wages, so it's only natural that I give my best whenever I represent the club. I've got no time whatsoever for people who don't try in the reserves. Having said that, I'd appreciate it more if I was involved with the first team.

FEBRUARY 15

Twelve Everton fans launch a "Goodison for Everton" campaign because they are worried at increasing speculation that we will move to a new ground. I don't know any more about this and at the moment I'm not bothered.

FEBRUARY 17

The club's sponsors, Danka, say they are going to pull out at the end of the season. They have decided not to extend their two-year backing by another two years. This does not reflect well on Everton. I guess Danka are not impressed by the way things are going for us. They are not the only ones.

FEBRUARY 18

Joe Royle bids £1.25 million for Bradford City's goalkeeper, Mark Schwarzer. I'm not really bothered by this, either, because I know the gaffer doesn't want me to hang around here. At least this will make sure I go.

Schwarzer did quite well against us in the Cup tie, but I think his price is high. I just wish that if Everton are going to sign somebody, they'd make it a player who will win us the League one day. I'm not necessarily talking about an outfield player. Let's think back to the Nigel Martyn episode. I've got a lot of time for Nigel—I think he's a very good goalkeeper. But would he have won us the League? Will Schwarzer win us the League? We need to buy the cream of the crop. I can't see the point in Royle replacing me with someone who will be doing exactly the same job. If someone is to replace me, then he needs to be better than me. It's as simple as that. Schwarzer is no better than me, so why go for him?

When Royle came here as manager, I looked at how he used his goalkeepers at Oldham. He used to swap Paul and John Hallworth around. Maybe he's intending to do the same at Everton. I'm not sure that's a good idea.

FEBRUARY 21

Mark Schwarzer signs for Middlesbrough. Oh, well. Joe Royle will have to try and buy someone else.

FEBRUARY 22

Coventry City v Everton
As a spectacle this is disgraceful. I feel sorry for our fans, who have travelled in numbers to Highfield Road and who give us tremendous backing. Once again, our squad is stretched—possibly more so now than at any time so far. Michael Ball, a left-sided player, is the latest teenager to be drafted onto the substitutes' bench.

We field a very defensive side, with five at the back, because we cannot afford to lose against another team who, like us, have their work cut out to avoid dropping out of the division. In a sense, a goalless draw is mission accomplished, but this match is such a non-event that

Craig Short's excellent first half tackle on the escaping Darren Huckerby just happens to be the highlight. Shorty hit the Coventry woodwork a few minutes earlier when he was inside the six-yard box, and it's clear from then that nobody is going to score today.

Paul Gerrard blocks from Huckerby after the break in a rare moment of excitement, before Steve Ogrizovic saves a Duncan Ferguson shot. I suppose considering the lack of action, this is the type of fixture every goalkeeper relishes. I'd still love to be out there, but I'm trying to make the most of my position at the moment. I'm studying closely how the gaffer and Willie Donachie work while I'm on the touchline because, in harbouring management ambitions, it's important I learn from others.

Coventry City 0 Everton 0
Gerrard; Barrett, Short, Watson, Unsworth, Phelan; Stuart, Thomsen, Speed; Ferguson, Barmby.
Subs (not used): Rideout, Branch, Allen, Ball, Southall.
Attendance: 19,497

FEBRUARY 25

John Hills has his loan spell at Swansea extended by another month.

FEBRUARY 26

John Ebbrell is transferred to Sheffield United for £1 million. This is a great move for him, especially as he will be linking up again with Howard Kendall and has a chance to play Premiership football next season. Howard always rated Ebbo when he was Everton's manager, and this is the kind of signing which could see United come up through the play-offs.

I have said before that John, like Alan Harper and Kevin Richardson here before him, is a players' player. These people may not excite the fans too much, but no side should be without them. Howard has done well. I wonder if Ebbo will be replaced.

Another player could be on the move. Paul Rideout has been offered a two-year contract by Japanese club Shimizu-F-Pulse, which is managed by former Spurs player Ossie Ardiles. I don't know how well Paul would take to the Orient, but the money would be good, I'm sure.

MARCH

		Pts
8	SHEFFIELD WED	39
9	LEEDS UTD	33
10	EVERTON	32
11	TOTTENHAM H	32
12	LEICESTER CITY	30

SATURDAY, MARCH 1

Everton v Arsenal

I'm back! No, not because Joe Royle has had a change of heart. It's more a case of his having no choice. I'm only playing because Paul Gerrard has strained a calf, and the only other alternative would be to use young James Speare, who has never been near the first team. Still, this will be a good experience for him, because he's on the bench.

Before the home games where I have been substitute, I've been going training in the morning and making my way to Goodison in the afternoon. Royle told me yesterday that it may not be a good idea for me to train this time because Paul was doubtful, but I said I still wanted to

Joe Parkinson is back for Craig Short as we attempt a more positive approach after the Coventry game. Arsenal aren't quite at full strength. They have David

Seaman, Steve Bould, Tony Adams and Paul Merson injured, while Ray Parlour is suspended. Names like Harper, Shaw and Rankin appear on their list of substitutes. Who are they?

I don't feel razor sharp and I can't help feeling that I'm under the spotlight. Fortunately the crowd give me a great ovation. At least they are behind me.

I'm given a rude welcome back to the Premiership when I come to collect David Platt's cross in the 13th minute and Earl Barrett clatters into me. My head is a bit sore, even after treatment, but I'm okay.

The bigger blow comes two minutes later. Nigel Winterburn hits a long ball forward which David Unsworth allows to bounce and Dennis Bergkamp runs through to score. Unzy is having a difficult first half. I feel sorry for him because nothing is going right and the fans are beginning to get on his back. Bergkamp and Ian Wright are pulling us all over the place and we are in total disarray.

I can't say I'm too surprised when Arsenal score a second goal. I've always been a big fan of Wright, and anyone who is at this match will see why. He brilliantly controls a pass from Remi Garde, turns away from Earl and hits a first time shot past me.

The frustration among the supporters boils over when the referee, Paul Danson, awards Arsenal a goal-kick when we clearly should have a corner. One angry fan runs onto the field to say his piece, although I can't make out whether he's having a go at Danson or Duncan Ferguson.

Unzy is replaced at half-time by Shorty, as much to spare him as to strengthen us, I think. Michael Branch is also on for Nick Barmby. At least we show some fight in this half. Gary Speed plants a free header wide from a corner and then Graham Stuart strikes a post when he has only John Lukic to beat. We think we have won a penalty when Branchy goes down in the area from Lukic's challenge, but Danson doesn't want to know.

The truth is, however, we don't do anything like enough to deserve even a point. Arsenal look a very strong side, and it's worrying to think they beat us comfortably without some of their key players.

I've counted at least eight bookings in this physical match. One of them just happens to be Speedo, who, we learn, has reached 21 disciplinary points and will be banned for one game. Just what we don't need.

Everton 0 Arsenal 2

Southall; Barrett, Watson (Short 46), Unsworth,
Phelan; Parkinson, Thomsen, Speed;
Barmby (Branch 46), Ferguson, Stuart.
Subs (not used): Hottiger, Rideout, Speare.
Attendance: 36,980

MARCH 3

A Frenchman, Laurent Viaud, comes to us on a week's trial. He's a midfielder from Monaco, but that's all I know about him. He speaks a bit of English and he seems a decent enough lad. But we won't know how good he is until he plays a game—assuming his club gives him clearance to do so. If it doesn't, then this is surely a pointless exercise—especially as the gaffer won't be able to see him for two days because we have a match at Southampton.

MARCH 4

The papers are linking Duncan with Aston Villa, who are supposed to be sniffing after Liverpool's Stan Collymore, too. Now that would be a hell of a strike force. On their day . . .

MARCH 5

Southampton v Everton
Neither team can afford to lose this game, and we are given an early warning when Matthew Le Tissier hits a swerving, long range drive which crashes against an upright. I am rooted to the spot—and very relieved. That

incident apart, we have settled better than Southampton, and Fergie's towering header from Nick Barmby's corner gives us an 11th minute lead.

Less than half an hour passes and we double our advantage from a move which begins with Earl Barrett. Claus and Nick are also involved before Earl overlaps and finds Gary Speed, who nets confidently. Earl is having his best attacking game for us here. He rampages down that right flank and Southampton don't know how to stop him. In first half stoppage time he looks certain to score when he cuts into the box, but he can only shoot weakly at Maik Taylor.

We are well in control, so it's no surprise Graeme Souness makes changes at half-time. He brings on Robbie Slater and Mickey Evans, and Slater makes his presence felt by firing a low shot past me just before the hour. Then it's comedy time as we crumble. Jason Dodd sends over a hopeful cross which I intend to claim. I call for the ball, but Craig Short beats me to it and heads into his own net.

Shorty tells me he heard my call but that he also heard Dave Watson shout "away!" so he tried to head the ball over the bar. I wish he'd tried to head over the bar in our game at Spurs because that way he might have scored! There's no point in having a go at Craig. We've got to concentrate on the rest of the game and make sure the next thing we both do is right. I don't believe in abusing people if they make a mistake. You see certain goalkeepers slaughtering their defenders constantly. I don't think that's necessarily a good thing; I don't think being shouted at means defenders give their keepers more respect. I reckon it has the opposite effect.

Taylor then saves Joe Parkinson's header before I stop a Le Tissier shot. But this is another game where we regard a draw as disappointing considering how things have gone in the first half.

Southampton 2 Everton 2

Southall; Barrett, Short, Watson, Unsworth, Phelan; Thomsen (Stuart 75), Parkinson, Speed; Ferguson, Barmby (Branch 81).
Subs not used: Rideout, Hottiger, Speare.

Attendance: 15,134

MARCH 6

We are linked with West Ham's Croatian defender, Slaven Bilic. With the transfer deadline approaching, I expect us to make a signing or two.

MARCH 7

Slaven Bilic asks to leave West Ham. I think we are definitely in for him.

MARCH 8

Leeds United v Everton

Elland Road is our bogey ground. It's been years since
Everton last won a League game there. What's more, it
will be especially hard to win today because I've read in
the Press that Leeds haven't conceded a home goal in the
Premiership since Boxing Day. That's George Graham for
you.

Graham brings back Carlton Palmer, who has been
linked with a move to Everton. I reckon he thinks he's
already with us because he plays the ball to Fergie and
Nigel Martyn has to save. Martyn has a fine game. It's
just as well, too, because we absolutely batter Leeds,
despite losing Joe Parkinson after seven minutes.

True, Gunnar Halle and Tony Yeboah miss chances
within seconds, but this looks like being our game. Just
as he was in the match at Goodison, Gary Speed is really
fired up. The Leeds fans boo him each time he touches
the ball and it's probably frustration which leads to an
early booking. Gary is already going to miss our game
against Derby later this month through suspension. I
have a feeling this yellow card will earn him another ban.
I hope I'm wrong.

Tony Phelan has a clear run on Martyn who parries
his shot when I think it's going to end up in the net. I,
meanwhile, don't have anything to do until the 27th
minute—when I have to pick the ball out of my net! Lee

Bowyer centres following a corner, and Robert Molenaar takes advantage of our slack marking to head in. That goal gives Leeds a boost, and I have to dive to save Brian Deane's diving header.

Early into the second half, Yeboah's snap-shot forces me to push the ball away. But then we start imposing ourselves again. Just before the hour, Unzy can't believe his luck when the ball lands at his feet from Duncan's header. However, he doesn't connect powerfully enough, and Martyn is able to save. We are relying a lot on Fergie's height and power at this stage, but we aren't giving him enough good service.

Michael Branch comes on as substitute, and has an excellent chance to grab the point we richly deserve as he sprints away from Speedo's long pass. But once again Martyn does well, spreading himself to stop the shot.

We are still around mid-table, although people are saying we could easily get sucked into a relegation fight. But I honestly don't think it will come to that. There is no way we will go down. We are too good for that. There is enough ability in the camp to keep us up. Anyone who doubts that should come and watch training every day. It's just a question of putting everything together—and coping with the pressure. I'm having no trouble doing that.

Rather than thinking of the possibility of relegation, I'm thinking that this is one game nearer the end of my Everton career.

Leeds United 1 Everton 0

Southall; Short (Rideout 82), Watson, Unsworth;
Barrett, Thomsen, Parkinson (Stuart 7), Speed,
Phelan; Ferguson, Barmby (Branch 59).
Subs (not used): Hottiger, Speare.

Attendance: 32,055

MARCH 10

Joe Royle confirms his interest in Slaven Bilic, who is
rated at £4.5 million. He wants to sign him before the
transfer deadline, which is March 27. We certainly need
more players.

MARCH 11

Slaven Bilic announces that he won't leave West Ham
until the end of the season. The whisper is, though, that
he'll be coming to us then.

MARCH 15

Everton v Derby County

Paul Gerrard is fit again, but strangely the man who
Joe Royle has made his first choice can only get on the

bench. Speedo is suspended, which suggests we won't be as potent going forward.

We have all the play in this match, but we don't trouble Martin Taylor once in the first half. In fact, the only moment of danger in that period comes from Aljosa Asanovic's cross which drifts dangerously towards my goal, and I have to back-pedal and push the ball over.

Because we are struggling to score, the boss brings on Graham Stuart in place of Michael Branch at half-time. But we fall into the usual trap of humping high balls towards Duncan. This tactic isn't working, and I don't think we are going to get a goal today. We are still too predictable. Teams come to Goodison with a plan to mark big Duncan, and if they can do that they know they have probably got us sussed. We need to show more guile and more imagination. Fortunately, something finally goes right for us 11 minutes from time as Duncan heads down for Waggy to rifle home an excellent shot from around 12 yards. We need this! Claus isn't so fortunate, however. He injures himself while celebrating the goal and has to be stretchered off.

It's still tight in the bottom half of the table. Some time ago I thought 50 points would be enough to ensure any side stayed up. Now, because teams are beating each other, I think 40 could be enough. We are only seven points off that target, with nine games to play.

Everton 1 Derby County 0

Southall; Short, Watson, Unsworth; Barrett,
Thomsen (Hottiger 79), Parkinson, Phelan;
Barmby; Branch (Stuart 46), Ferguson.
Subs (not used): Rideout, Dunne, Gerrard.

Attendance: 32,140

MARCH 18

The papers say we are now chasing QPR winger Trevor
Sinclair. So let's get him.

MARCH 20

Paul Rideout, whose move to Japan didn't materialise, is
offered the chance to play in China. A club called Huan
Dao Vanguards in a place called Chongqing has agreed
to pay Everton £250,000 for him.

What is it with Ridders and the Orient? I reckon he
should go for this one because I believe he'll be on good
money over there, tax free. At this stage of his career, he
won't be able to earn that kind of wage here . . . unless
he plays for at least another four years. All he has to do
to secure his transfer is prove to the Chinese that he can
run two miles and 80 yards inside 12 minutes. Piece of
cake! Think of the cash, mate!

Paul deserves a break like this. He's a good pro, and

whatever he does now he'll be remembered by Evertonians for scoring the winning goal in the 1995 FA Cup final against Manchester United. On that basis alone he should have a good move.

Mind you, I'd be sorry to see him go because I like him and because we'd be losing another good player. At the moment there don't seem to be many coming in! And the transfer deadline is a week away.

MARCH 22

Everton v Manchester United
That's better! After keeping a clean sheet against Derby, I now find myself back on the bench. I can't understand the logic of dropping me, even though the news didn't entirely come as a shock because Paul Gerrard is definitely fit for this game.

Nevertheless, I still asked the manager for an explanation. "I want to build for the future," he said. He also blamed me for the second goal Arsenal scored at Goodison earlier this month. He says nothing at the time, but he mentions it now, which I find rather strange.

I tell him: "I've got no future, then, have I?" He says: "I want you to stay and fight for your place with Paul." But if he is building for the future and Gez is playing because he's younger, what future can I have at 38? It's in my best interests to leave the club as soon as possible, because I'm definitely not going to get another game while Royle is here.

I don't want to leave, but I'm being forced to. All I've wanted is to play my last game and let it be known it will be my last game, but it doesn't look as though I will be given that opportunity.

Gary Speed is back after suspension and, after the non-eventful first half hour we fancy our chances because United aren't too spectacular—and Terry Phelan is having a great game. He stands out because of his speed and fitness. But we go behind in the 34th minute—against the run of play—to a goal out of nothing.

Ole Gunnar Solksjaer receives the ball around the edge of the area with his back to goal. He turns Waggy well and fires a low shot which creeps inside Gerrard's near post. I feel sorry for Paul. It may look better for me if he has a dodgy game, but I don't want that. Paul isn't helped by our defence not playing well. Mind you, we should have a penalty in the 37th minute when Ronny Johnsen—a substitute for Gary Pallister—holds back Diamond in the area.

Paul Rideout, whom we expect to head off for China after this game, replaces Claus Thomsen—who has been struggling with injury—at half time. It's only then that the boss decides to do something about Eric Cantona, who has dropped off the front line and has been pulling us about. Surely this should have been sorted out before the game. Another blunder. Cantona still manages to find enough space to release Roy Keane, only for Gez to dive at his feet.

Paul also does well to block David Beckham's volley, but all hope of an equaliser is lost in the 78th minute when Paul fails to claim a Beckham cross, and collides with Earl Barrett, leaving Cantona free to stroke the ball home. I chat to Paul after the game—he's going to keep his head up.

United will be relieved with the result. They are now six points clear of Liverpool. We, on the other hand, aren't guaranteed safety, but we should be. The bottom three—Southampton, Nottingham Forest and Coventry —don't look too clever . . . and they are running out of games.

Everton 0 Manchester United 2
Gerrard; Barrett, Watson, Unsworth, Phelan;
Thomsen (Rideout 46), Parkinson, Barmby,
Speed; Ferguson, Stuart.
Subs (not used): Short, Hottiger, Branch, Southall.
Attendance: 40,079

MARCH 26

Chelsea come in for me. They are prepared to offer me nearly twice the money that I'm on now, plus an 18-month contract. This would be my last contract, too. I'm well happy. I telephone Joe Royle to see what the situation is and I can't believe it when he tells me I can't go! What is this guy trying to do to me?

He says he has been trying to sign all sorts of goal-keepers, but hasn't been able to bring one to the club, so he needs me here. You could say we have a heated debate. It's the first time he has ever raised his voice to me. He sounds tired and fed up. Our conversation ends with him putting the phone down on me.

Royle wants to sign two Norwegians from SK Brann, Claus Eftevaag and Tore Andre Flo, before tomorrow's deadline. Barry Horne is also waiting for a phone call because Royle wants him back from Birmingham as a player/coach.

MARCH 27

There's never a dull moment here. Joe Royle resigns! I feel a bit sorry for him because it's evident the pressure has got to him. That was clear from our last phone conversation. Looking back, he should have taken more days off to get away from the pressure. That has contributed to his downfall.

I don't think Everton has been too big for Royle. He just needed to understand the pressures which surround such a big club. It's completely different to Oldham. There, success was survival. Here, you have to do a lot more than survive. Everton should be like Barcelona. The fact that we are not gets everyone down.

Joe's public relations haven't been the best. At a club like Everton it should be a case of everyone working for the common cause. He made a mistake in banning the Press recently from our Bellefield training ground. When you do things like that you immediately drive a wedge between yourself and the media. That's a dangerous game to play, and I think Royle has realised that. If you make enemies with the media, you make enemies for life. They'll be waiting for him to take another job so they can hammer him again.

This is why I admire Alex Ferguson, and Kenny Dalglish when he was in charge of Liverpool. Kenny never said much, but he would always give credit to his team. I think we could have done with a bit more of that this season.

Although Joe has caused me problems lately, I've never wanted him to lose his job. However, I do feel a bit frustrated because if he was going to resign, why couldn't he have let me go to Chelsea? I'm surprised he has quit. I expected him to see the job through at least until the end of the season. Now is not the best time to leave the club. No matter how tough a job is, you should stick with it.

It appears the reason he has gone is because the chairman has blocked his moves for Barry Horne and the Norwegian players. I'm hearing there was some sort of cash wrangle regarding Flo and his previous club. If the gaffer believes he won't be allowed to manage the club the way he wants to, then I guess I can understand him doing what he has. In that sense he has made a brave decision. But from a selfish point of view I'm very annoyed. I feel let down. I feel he has gone purely for his own benefit. Barry is destroyed when he hears the news because it means his move back to Everton is off.

I haven't a clue who the next manager will be, but Waggy is appointed caretaker until the end of the season. Willie Donachie has agreed to stay on and help him. I'm happy with this—whether I play or not.

MARCH 29

Wales v Belgium

Belgium aren't one of the world's most powerful football nations these days, but even they are too good for us.

Their right-back, Bertrand Crasson, opens the scoring with a cracker. He beats Ryan Giggs, goes past Mark Pembridge and hits a long-range drive which flies past me and goes in off the underside of the bar. If he meant that, then it was some goal!

But we let ourselves down on the stroke of half-time by giving Lorenzo Staelens a free header which virtually kills the game, and which brings boos from the Cardiff crowd as we head to the dressing room.

Bobby Gould switches Giggsy to the right wing in the second half, and we definitely improve. The introduction of John Hartson for Dean Saunders gives us something extra, and Gary Speed, who again plays well as sweeper, heads home a corner in the 67th minute. Unfortunately it's not enough.

Meanwhile, over at Goodison, the guessing games start as to the identity of our new manager. Already Bobby Robson is being tipped for the job.

Wales 1 Belgium 2

Southall; Blackmore, Pembridge, Symons, Page, V. Jones, Horne, Speed, Saunders (Hartson 64), M. Hughes, Giggs.

Attendance: 15,000

MARCH 31

Jurgen Klinsmann is linked with our manager's job. Well, as a player/manager to be precise. We're not paying any attention to these rumours because we're not looking beyond this season. We know that Dave Watson is in charge for the moment and that's all we're concerned about. Waggy has every right to feel nervous, but he has the backing of all the staff.

APRIL

		Pts
11	LEICESTER CITY	39
12	BLACKBURN R	36
13	EVERTON	36
14	MIDDLESBROUGH	35
15	DERBY COUNTY	35

FRIDAY, APRIL 4

Dave Watson says that because of our depleted squad he intends recalling Paul Rideout from China—just before he signs over there for his new club. I wonder how he'll like that!

APRIL 5

Aston Villa v Everton
Waggy recalls me for his first game in charge, and we are down to the bare bones. Earl Barrett, who has played in every game this season, is injured and he joins Andy Hinchcliffe, Nick Barmby, Tony Grant and Jon O'Connor on the sidelines.

A Savo Milosevic shot, which I save, is all I have to do in the opening half hour or so as we play some good football and take the game to Villa. We try to build from the back on occasions, thereby mixing up our play, and even though we look defensively shaky at times, it seems to be working.

With Mark Bosnich injured, Michael Oakes keeps goal for Villa and he performs exceptionally. He makes an outstanding reflex save to deny Graham Stuart. Soon after, he does it again, although this time Diamond is better placed to score. In the 13th minute, following the corner, Unzy sees Oakes pull off another wonder save, but he is able to react quickly and knock the rebound into the net.

Unfortunately we concede a goal at just the wrong moment—four minutes before half-time. We fail to clear a corner, and when the ball is played to the unmarked Milosevic at the far post, he directs a simple header home.

Five minutes into the second half we go behind from Steve Staunton's brilliant free-kick, which he curls around our wall. This annoys me because I put Marc Hottiger on the post for protection, but he ran off it and that helped Staunton find the way though. If he'd stayed there, he wouldn't have scored. Now we are in trouble. Milosevic then causes me problems with a snap-shot which I have to push over and in the 53rd minute he sends over a cross aimed at Ugo Ehiogu. The ball falls to Dwight Yorke, who is unmarked, and he scores Villa's third goal. Three goals conceded in 13 minutes: that's capitulation for you!

It's only when there are seven minutes remaining that

we test Oakes again, but he is equal to Claus Thomsen's spectacular shot. Waggy and I have a chat after the game and we decide that in future we need someone we can trust to cover the post on free-kicks. Waggy will do it himself.

Aston Villa 3 Everton 1

Southall; Short, Watson, Unsworth (Dunne 59); Hottiger (Branch 54), Thomsen, Parkinson, Speed, Phelan; Ferguson, Stuart. Subs (not used): Ball, Hills, Gerrard. Attendance: 39,339

APRIL 9

Everton v Leicester City

We are under no illusions about how hard this game will be. We already know that Leicester are no pushovers and they, like us, need points, even though their position is safer than ours. We have to win this game.

Dave Watson drops Marc and Claus. Michael Branch and Nick Barmby are back, and Branchy looks lively from the start. He scores his first goal at Goodison in the 16th minute by neatly converting Duncan Ferguson's header down. Our football is good; we are enterprising, imaginative and showing plenty of movement, and Kasey Keller makes saves from Nick and Craig Short.

But half-time seems to do something to us. We tend to

play much better in the first period than in the second, and this match is the perfect example. Much as we are good before the break, we are well and truly battered after it. Possibly the turnaround is explained by the knee injury to Joe Parkinson, which forces his withdrawal at half-time. It looks painful and there are fears he might not be able to play again this season. I hope he can, because we really do need him. We are going to play some really tough games and he is ideal for that.

Steve Guppy and Muzzy Izzet come close for Leicester. But Matt Elliott is even closer with a header which hits the inside of the post, and I have to pat the ball away. Emile Heskey then fires narrowly wide and we can all sense the inevitable. It happens in the 69th minute when Ian Marshall beats me with a powerful volley.

There is no escaping the fact that this is a bad result. But I can't stress the importance of remaining positive. One point is better than none, and at least it means we can add to our total. It just makes Saturday's home game against Spurs even more vital. I'm still confident we won't go down. If we beat Spurs, then we're almost home and dry.

Everton 1 Leicester City 1

Southall; Short, Watson, Unsworth; Stuart, Parkinson (Thomsen 46), Speed, Phelan; Barmby (Hottiger 75); Ferguson, Branch.
Subs (not used): Ball, Dunne, Gerrard.
Attendance: 30,368

APRIL 12

Everton v Tottenham Hotspur

Earl Barrett has recovered from the knee injury which forced him out of the two previous matches, but Craig Short and David Unsworth have both failed morning fitness tests. This means another reshuffle, with Paul Rideout—back from China—having to operate in midfield. It's his first start since the game at Sheffield Wednesday in January.

Ridders plays well again, and it's his ball which finds Graham Stuart down the right in the 10th minute. He beats Justin Edinburgh and crosses for Gary Speed to power a brilliant header past Ian Walker. We have scored some great goals this season. This is Gary's 11th. I believe he's never got more than 12, so this just shows what a good buy he has been.

Ridders and Diamond test Ian Walker, but Fergie should do better when Waggy's pass gives him a run on goal. I can't believe how weakly he shoots at Walker. The only save I have to make in the first half is from Allan Nielsen's close range header. I'm pleased with it.

We have to make a half-time change by bringing on young Michael Ball, an England Youth international, for Terry Phelan, who, I think, has injured his knee. Michael settles in well and can be proud of his performance. It's not an easy game to play because of the pressure and because Spurs look more threatening in the second half, but he does fine. It's good to see so many youngsters getting their chance this season—and taking it. Sol Campbell plants a header wide when he's well-placed, but that's the only thing he didn't do right. What a player he is! He's got power and energy—and he gets everywhere. We react well with Walker tipping Diamond's 25-yarder over the bar and Speedo's header being hacked off the line.

It's just as well Waggy has decided he will cover the near post on free-kicks because he comes to our rescue after Diamond fouls Jason Dozzell. Dave isn't exactly standing on the goal-line when Teddy Sheringham prepares to take the kick because he doesn't want to play people onside. Instead, he's standing just off the wall. Well, he's in the right place, because the ball hits him on the chest and there is an almighty scramble during which I make a reflex save. But don't ask me who from! Spurs apply a great deal of pressure and we do well to resist, not least when our caretaker manager heads another chance off the line.

We have shown guts today. It's been our Cup final and we've won it. There are a lot of happy and relieved people around afterwards, including, of course, the supporters who have been magnificent. They have helped us a lot.

Everton 1 Tottenham Hotspur 0

Southall; Barrett, Watson, Dunne; Stuart,
Rideout, Thomsen, Speed, Phelan (Ball 46);
Ferguson, Branch (Barmby 57).
Subs (not used): Hottiger, Hills, Gerrard.

Attendance: 36,380

APRIL 14

Paul Rideout, who was injured against Spurs, heads back
to China to complete his move.

APRIL 15

The club denies reports of an interest in Francesco
Moriero, who is a winger with Roma. I've never heard of
him.

APRIL 16

Everton v Liverpool

We know that if we win this game we will not only fend
off any lingering fears of the drop, we will also seriously
damage Liverpool's Championship hopes. Two great
reasons, then, for giving it our best shot—quite apart
from local pride, which is always at stake in derbies.

I'm a bit surprised—and pleased—that Jason McAteer isn't playing. I reckon he could have caused us problems down our left flank. That said, things begin badly for us anyway. Robbie Fowler makes a back for Craig Short, who lands awkwardly and he has to go off after just 22 minutes. We already have two teenagers starting this game—Richard Dunne and Michael Branch—and we are forced to count on another when we bring on Michael Ball. As against Tottenham, he is completely unfazed by the occasion.

Liverpool are playing well. In fact, they have the better of things for over an hour. Fowler and Steve McManaman exchange passes well around our box and McManaman crosses for Jamie Redknapp to poke the ball past me off Claus Thomsen in the 26th minute. They deserve their lead because they are murdering us. We've got a good derby record over the last few years, but I think it's going to end tonight. If Liverpool score again we've definitely had it.

Waggy changes a few things at half-time. We decide to get closer on McManaman and deny him space. There is no doubt we improve in the second half. Duncan Ferguson, who is having a tremendous battle with Bjorn Tore Kvarme, scores a wonderful equaliser when he turns and fires a low shot past David James from the edge of the area.

Liverpool hit back, creating three chances inside 60 seconds. Redknapp forces me to save his low drive, then

Fowler heads against our bar and clips the side of a post with a shot. However, we are far from finished, because Michael Thomas nods a Ferguson header off the line and then James reacts smartly to push away Claus' rising drive.

Because of the importance of this match, tempers spill over, with Fowler and David Unsworth being sent off for fighting eight minutes from time. This will probably go down as dangerous play in the referees' report, which means both players would get a three-match ban. Unzy has gone in hard on Fowler. Fowler has seen him coming on the next occasion and whacked him. Unzy has hit him back and it started a bit of a scuffle. This sort of thing is going to happen in derby games. I think Stephen Lodge, the referee, might have been a bit more lenient. It's pointless to send them off. A good talking-to, and a yellow card each, would surely be a more sensible form of punishment. If the referee had spotted Unzy's first tackle on Fowler then he would have been penalised and none of this would have happened.

In the end, we deserve our draw, which is yet another example of how we can lift ourselves against the strong teams. We've beaten Newcastle, drawn at Manchester United and drawn twice with Liverpool. On the face of it, that's quite impressive. It's the other results which have let us down.

Everton 1 Liverpool 1

Southall; Short (Ball 22), Watson, Dunne;
Barrett, Stuart, Thomsen (Barmby 63), Speed,
Unsworth; Ferguson, Branch.
Subs (not used): Hottiger, Hills, Gerrard.

Attendance: 40,177.

APRIL 19

West Ham v Everton

We may have played more League games than any
other team in the Premiership—this is our 36th—but if
we manage a draw today we'll have 42 points, which
should definitely do us. Michael Ball is given his full
debut because Terry Phelan is still injured, while Richard
Dunne—who has, incredibly, been called into the full
Republic of Ireland squad—performed so well against
Liverpool that he keeps his place.

West Ham skipper Julian Dicks is out injured, but they
aren't missing him as they go ahead in the ninth minute.
Steve Lomas launches a high throw into our box. I can
only lay one hand on the ball, which is not enough, and
it drops perfectly for Paul Kitson to hammer home. West
Ham are playing with their tails up and Kitson misses a
chance to increase their lead when he shoots past me—
and also past the far post.

However, he's at it again in the 32nd minute, converting Michael Hughes' backward ball, and we are in deep

trouble. We haven't even forced Ludek Miklosko into a notable save. The half-time appearance of Nick Barmby for Ball changes the game for us, but not before West Ham are awarded a 49th minute penalty for Dunny's trip on Hugo Porfirio. With Dicks not playing, I might have a chance of saving this. John Hartson is given the ball. He's obviously been told to take the pens today, but he offers it to Kitson so he can complete his hat-trick. The act of sentiment backfires because he hits the ball too high and I parry it away. I normally dive to the right but this time, for some reason, I go left—and I'm pleased I do!

Nick is very inventive. His passing and movement is great and West Ham can't contain him. It's from his 76th minute cross that we pull a goal back, Duncan Ferguson heading down for Michael Branch to dart in and nod the ball over the line. We press hard for an equaliser and we are deep into stoppage time when Nick's free-kick tempts Miklosko off his line, and Fergie stretches out his right foot to volley home superbly. Just desserts again. We appear to be getting the breaks these days.

West Ham 2 Everton 2
Southall; Dunne, Watson, Unsworth; Barrett, Stuart, Thomsen, Speed, Ball (Barmby 46); Ferguson, Branch.
Subs (not used): Hottiger, O'Connor, Hills, Gerrard.
Attendance: 24,525

APRIL 23

Waggy tells the Press that we need at least eight new players to get a good squad strength for next season. He's right, but it's no good buying stop-gap players. If we are going to spend money, then we should spend it on quality. But how have we been allowed to be left with such a depleted squad? Joe Royle let quite a few people go, but how many did he replace? There is absolutely no way we should have found ourselves in this situation.

APRIL 30

Peter Johnson reveals that he has drawn up a short-list of four for the manager's job here. Bobby Robson and three others, I suppose.

MAY

		Pts
10	LEEDS UTD	44
11	DERBY COUNTY	43
12	EVERTON	42
13	BLACKBURN R	41
14	LEICESTER CITY	40

FRIDAY, MAY 2

Inter Milan's Paul Ince tells *The Sun* that he would like to join Everton. That's the type of player we should be looking for. It would be nice if Ince came to us, not just because he is a quality midfielder but also to show people once and for all that we are not a racist club. Even though we've got black players here, we still get labelled as racist. I'm sick and tired of hearing this. We never have been, we certainly aren't now and we never will be.

I'm not convinced by Ince's words, though. I think this is more a case of his trying to stir up interest among other clubs than an out-and-out plea to come to Goodison. Still, it's nice for our fans to see someone saying they want to sign for us.

You could ask how it is that we could sign any player when we haven't got a manager. Well, my information is that we've as good as got Slaven Bilic already, so anything is possible. He played quite well against us the other week and should be a good long-term signing.

MAY 3

Sunderland v Everton
When you have lost more games at Roker Park—38—than any other team, and when you are the last opponents to play an official game there before Sunderland move to a new stadium, you know things aren't going to be easy.

This is a difficult day for us, made more so by the officiating of referee Keith Burge and his assistants. We are not short of confidence going into this game. Nick Barmby's performance at West Ham has earned him a start, while Terry Phelan is also back. David Unsworth, who is suspended, and Michael Ball, drop out. Sunderland aren't too menacing in the first half. In fact, we don't do badly, with Lionel Perez saving superbly from Fergie and then blocking at Branchy's feet. I have nothing to do.

But in the 35th minute things start to go wrong for us. Duncan is pushed in the back when he jumps for a cross in his own box, and the ball connects with his arm. Incredibly, Burge ignores that shove and awards Sunderland a penalty for handball. If the referee has considered this to be deliberate handball, then Fergie should be sent off. But if he's not been dismissed then why award a penalty in the first place? I dive the right way, but Paul Stewart's shot is too powerful and we find ourselves trailing in a game where we could have been ahead.

Sunderland introduce Allan Johnston for Gareth Hall at half-time, and they benefit from another controversial decision in the 56th minute when Burge penalises me for stepping out of the box when clearing the ball. This is an outrageous decision! It's the referee's assistant who has attracted Burge's attention, signalling I used my foot to kick the ball outside the area. That happens to be in the rules. Once again, justice isn't done as Chris Waddle blasts the free-kick, which takes a deflection off Gary Speed's shoulder, and the ball flies into the net. I'm rooted to the spot. I'm fed up of Waddle. As much as I like him, after what he did for Bradford I'm sick of him scoring against Everton this season. But he's one of those players who deserves what he gets from football. We could have done with signing someone like him to gee the lads up until the end of the season.

Waddle is involved in Sunderland's third goal, curling over a cross from the left which the unmarked Johnston heads in at the far post in the 68th minute. Phelan has to leave the field injured four minutes from the end and is replaced by John Hills who, because of our squad situation, has been prevented from extending his loan period at Swansea.

This is a hugely disappointing result, made even more so by the fact that two refereeing decisions have cost us the game rather than our own mistakes. Sunderland, like fellow strugglers Middlesbrough, have beaten us twice this season. That's not something we should feel proud of. Amazingly, we still haven't assured our place in the Premiership for next season. Nottingham Forest are already down and Coventry are unable to catch us, but we still have to worry about the third relegation place. Middlesbrough are the danger. They are six points behind us with two games in hand, and they are three goals better off. If they hadn't had three points deducted for not turning up at Blackburn we'd be right in the mire. I can't believe we are entering the last week of the season thinking about the drop. How has it all come to this?

'Boro have it tough. They've got to go to Old Trafford and Blackburn before next weekend. If they pick up at least three points, we'll be sweating against Chelsea next Sunday when, because of our injury problems, we might have to be relying on kids.

Sunderland 3 Everton 0

Southall; Barrett, Watson, Dunne, Phelan (Hills 86);
Stuart (Ball 73), Thomsen, Speed; Barmby;
Ferguson, Branch.
Subs (not used): Hottiger, O'Connor, Gerrard.
Attendance: 22,108

MAY 5

It's a Bank Holiday, and I'm in Chester. One bloke comes up to me and says: "Ha! Ha! You'd better win on Sunday, now!" He tells me Middlesbrough are 3-1 up at Manchester United and for the first time I admit that I think we are in serious danger of going down. I mean, if 'Boro can beat United at Old Trafford then think of the boost they will get. I thought United would hammer them. Middlesbrough, if they hold on, will certainly be capable of getting at least a point against Blackburn on Thursday and even something from their final game.

I drive home listening to the rest of the match on the radio, and I can tell you I am hugely relieved when United pull back to 3-3. A point for 'Boro is still more than I thought they'd get, so it's important for us they don't beat Blackburn. A draw for them, and we'd mathematically be safe.

MAY 6

Peter Johnson unveils plans for a 60,000-capacity new Goodison Park, to be built a few miles away from the present ground, at a cost of around £100 million. I know this is causing quite a debate in the city, but I think we've *got* to have a new stadium.

The facilities around Goodison at the moment aren't

fantastic. I find it much more comfortable to watch a game at Leeds than I do here because their facilities are superior and Elland Road is better situated than Goodison. If you've ever tried to drive away from our ground quickly after a game, you'll have realised it's impossible. A new stadium would alleviate all transport problems as well as providing better facilities.

The important thing is not to skimp on this project. For example, Middlesbrough's Riverside Stadium is nice, but they haven't done the dressing rooms properly; it's whitewash over breeze block. I don't think that's right for a top-class club. After all, you have to build towards a Super League. It's going to happen whether we like it or not—and Everton have to aim for that.

While I'd like to think we'll be getting a fantastic stadium, I hope all our money doesn't go into that without any consideration for team rebuilding. The fans must be worried about that. I'm sure they would much rather have money spent on the team than on a new ground.

MAY 8

Thankfully, we can go into the game against Chelsea free from pressure as Blackburn hold Middlesbrough to a goalless draw. That point ensures Blackburn's survival, as well as ours.

MAY 11

Everton v Chelsea

It's just as well we don't need anything from this match because I'm not sure we would get it. Just look at our bench for a start. Okay, Paul Gerrard is there, but unless you are a die-hard Evertonian, you wouldn't have heard of our other substitutes, Jon O'Connor, Danny Cadamarteri, Adam Eaton and Gavin McCann. Our squad is as bare as the female streaker who comes on in the second half.

We give John Hills his full debut, while Richard Dunne and Michael Ball complete the line-up of teenagers. All these lads are good players, but I doubt they would have had the necessary experience if this fixture had assumed greater importance.

Dennis Wise puts Chelsea ahead in the 13th minute with a great chip from Roberto Di Matteo's pass. Eight minutes later Dunny finds Duncan Ferguson, who is body-checked outside the box by Frode Grodas. It's a sending off offence, and the Chelsea keeper walks. Kevin Hitchcock comes on to replace him at the expense of Gianluca Vialli.

Ten minutes before half-time, Dan Petrescu sends over a right wing cross for Di Matteo to score with a header. We may be two goals down to a side with 10 men but, considering our lack of experience, we are doing quite well. Some people are shouting at us to get a grip, but what the hell do they want? We are playing against next week's FA Cup finalists with a bunch of kids and, while Chelsea cause us problems, we are not being overrun. We threaten again in the 40th minute, but Hitchcock saves from Dave Watson's header.

Waggy sends on lively young right-winger Cadamarteri at half-time in place of Claus Thomsen and we improve. Fergie heads a centre from Hills off target when he is unmarked, and then Marc Hottiger shoots off target from Fergie's through ball.

We finally get some reward in the 78th minute when Waggy heads Hills' corner powerfully towards goal. Hitchcock makes a fine save, but the ball drops kindly for Nick Barmby who knocks it into the net.

True, this is yet another home defeat, but I am made up with the performance of our young lads. The present may not be too great, but at least the future promises to be better. I hope to be a part of it for a couple more years, but I'll have to wait and see. . . .

Everton 1 Chelsea 2
Southall; Barrett, Watson, Dunne, Ball;
Hottiger, Thomsen (Cadamarteri 46),
Speed, Hills; Barmby, Ferguson.
Subs (not used): O'Connor, Eaton, McCann, Gerrard.
Attendance: 38,321

REFLECTIONS

		Pts
13	BLACKBURN R	42
14	WEST HAM UTD	42
15	EVERTON	42
16	SOUTHAMPTON	41
17	COVENTRY CITY	41

AT THE END OF THE DAY . . .

Our FA Cup win in 1995 had given everyone here false hope. We all knew it would be hard to make what many thought would be a natural progression, but we looked to be getting there by finishing in the top six in 1995/96.

Understandably, we began this season with even more optimism. But, with hindsight, our squad was way too small, and we didn't have a recognised goal-scorer. What's more, when Joe Royle sold Andrei Kanchelskis he didn't bother to replace him. He also tried to sign three keepers, ending up with one, but he failed to buy an out-and-out striker to partner Duncan Ferguson. Basically, he just got it wrong.

I have to say, however, that in the first two games we were only a fraction off being a very good side. There is no specific reason why everything went downhill afterwards, but with only 44 goals scored in our 38 League games it's evident we needed more fire-power.

If Joe had bought a striker who could score 20 goals a season we wouldn't have been in such a mess. We would have beaten Manchester United and many more teams as well. We might even have finished in Europe.

Look at Newcastle. They have been slaughtered for having a dodgy defence, but fair play to them: they finished second by scoring over 70 goals. Someone like Les Ferdinand would have done us fine, but my personal choice would have been Ian Wright. This guy guarantees you goals. He's the type of player who, when you are under the cosh, has the ability to break forward and sneak one which wins games you look like losing.

I know what you're thinking: there is no way Arsenal, who were going for the Championship, would have even considered selling him—unless they were offered loads of cash. If it means paying over the odds, then do it. Would it have been worth it in the long run to make Arsenal an offer they just couldn't refuse? I think so. I don't care how old Wright is. He is fit enough and good enough to get goals in the Premiership for at least the next two years. You're not going to tell me he wouldn't hit it off with Duncan Ferguson.

Fergie, though, is not the finished article yet. He's a great player, but he has to learn consistency. In his defence, I failed to see the point in fielding a 6' 4" striker if, after the sale of Kanchelskis, we had no-one to play the ball to him in the right areas. If we aren't going to use Duncan's strengths, then there's no point in his being out there.

On a personal level, I can sum things up this way: when I started the season I felt great; when I finished it I felt awful.

It's been suggested to me that perhaps I'm someone who refuses to accept that his career is coming to an end. I'm not—because it isn't! How about this then? I'll put my record of mistakes against anyone else's in the League. I judge myself on my number of mistakes. You tell me how many I made in this season compared to Peter Schmeichel and David James. I think you'll find it's very, very close.

This season will go down as the worst I've experienced as a professional footballer—because I was good enough for Chelsea and I was good enough for my country, but I wasn't good enough for Everton. You don't know how much that hurt.

I really felt let down when Joe Royle resigned. The more I thought about it the more I thought he should have had the guts to see the job through to the end of the season. When I was out of the team I was prepared to train hard, play in the reserves and give my all for Everton until May. Joe's leaving left so many people in limbo.

I hope that in the not too distant future Everton will

have put all their troubles behind them, and that they will again hold the position of pride and respectability they deserve. With or without Neville Southall.

POSTSCRIPT

Dave Watson continued as caretaker manager until the end of the season. Howard Kendall was appointed as manager on 27 June 1997. On 9 August 1997, Neville Southall made his 738th appearance for Everton, against Crystal Palace at Goodison Park, to begin his 17th season at the club.

APPENDIX A

1996/97 Season
Carling Premiership League
Positions—Month by Month

F. A. Carling Premiership
League Table—31 August 1996

		Plyd	W	D	L	For	Agt	W	D	L	For	Agt	GD	Pts
			HOME					**AWAY**						
1.	Sheffield Wed	3	1	0	0	2	1	2	0	0	4	1	+4	9
2.	Chelsea	3	2	0	0	3	0	0	1	0	0	0	+3	7
3.	Arsenal	3	1	0	0	2	0	1	0	1	2	2	+2	6
4.	Aston Villa	3	2	0	0	3	0	0	0	1	1	2	+2	6
5.	Manchester U	3	0	2	0	4	4	1	0	0	3	0	+3	5
6.	Sunderland	3	0	1	0	0	0	1	1	0	4	1	+3	5
7.	Liverpool	3	1	1	0	2	0	0	1	0	3	3	+2	5
8.	Everton	3	1	0	0	2	0	0	2	0	2	2	+2	5
9.	Tottenham H	3	0	2	0	1	1	1	0	0	2	0	+2	5
10.	Nottingham F	3	0	1	1	2	5	1	0	0	3	0	0	4
11.	Leeds Utd	3	1	0	1	1	2	0	1	0	3	3	-1	4
12.	West Ham U	3	1	1	0	3	2	0	0	1	0	2	-1	4
13.	Leicester City	3	1	0	1	2	3	0	1	0	0	0	-1	4
14.	Newcastle Utd	3	1	0	1	3	2	0	0	1	0	2	-1	3
15.	Middlesbrough	3	0	1	0	3	3	0	1	1	1	2	-1	2
16.	Derby County	3	0	1	0	3	3	0	1	1	1	3	-2	2
17.	Southampton	3	0	1	0	0	0	0	0	2	2	4	-2	1
18.	Blackburn R	3	0	0	1	0	2	0	1	1	2	3	-3	1
19.	Coventry City	3	0	0	1	0	3	0	1	1	1	3	-5	1
20.	Wimbledon	3	0	0	1	0	3	0	0	2	0	3	-6	0

F. A. Carling Premiership
League Table—30 September 1996

		Plyd	HOME					AWAY					GD	Pts
			W	D	L	For	Agt	W	D	L	For	Agt		
1.	Liverpool	8	3	1	0	9	2	3	1	0	9	4	+12	20
2.	Newcastle Utd	8	3	0	1	9	6	3	0	1	5	4	+4	18
3.	Arsenal	8	3	1	0	11	4	2	1	1	6	4	+9	17
4.	Manchester U	8	2	2	0	10	5	2	2	0	8	1	+12	16
5.	Wimbledon	8	3	0	1	8	4	2	0	2	4	3	+5	15
6.	Chelsea	8	2	2	0	5	2	1	2	1	6	8	+1	13
7.	Sheffield Wed	8	2	1	1	4	4	2	0	2	5	7	-2	13
8.	Aston Villa	8	2	2	0	5	2	1	1	2	6	7	+2	12
9.	Middlesbrough	8	2	1	1	11	6	1	1	2	3	7	+1	11
10.	Leicester City	8	2	0	2	3	6	1	2	1	3	3	-3	11
11.	Derby County	8	1	2	1	5	6	1	2	1	3	4	-2	10
12.	Sunderland	8	1	2	1	2	2	1	1	2	4	4	0	9
13.	Everton	8	2	0	2	5	3	0	3	1	3	7	-2	9
14.	Tottenham H	8	0	2	2	3	5	2	0	2	3	3	-2	8
15.	West Ham U	8	1	1	2	4	6	1	1	2	3	6	-5	8
16.	Nottingham F	8	0	2	2	2	7	1	2	1	7	7	-5	7
17.	Leeds Utd	8	1	0	3	1	7	1	1	2	5	6	-7	7
18.	Southampton	8	1	2	1	6	3	0	0	4	4	9	-2	5
19.	Coventry City	8	1	1	2	2	5	0	1	3	1	8	-10	5
20.	Blackburn R	8	0	1	3	2	6	0	2	2	3	5	-6	3

F. A. Carling Premiership
League Table—31 October 1996

		Plyd	W	D	L	For	Agt	W	D	L	For	Agt	GD	Pts
			HOME					*AWAY*						
1.	Arsenal	11	4	2	0	14	4	3	1	1	8	4	+14	24
2.	Newcastle Utd	11	4	0	1	14	6	4	0	2	6	6	+8	24
3.	Liverpool	10	4	1	0	11	3	3	1	1	9	5	+12	23
4.	Wimbledon	11	4	0	1	12	6	3	1	2	8	5	+9	22
5.	Manchester U	11	3	2	0	11	5	2	2	2	11	12	+5	19
6.	Chelsea	11	3	2	1	10	7	2	2	1	9	9	+3	19
7.	Aston Villa	11	3	2	0	7	2	1	1	4	6	9	+2	15
8.	Everton	10	3	0	2	7	4	1	3	1	4	7	0	15
9.	Sheffield Wed	11	2	2	1	5	5	2	1	3	7	11	-4	15
10.	Tottenham H	11	1	2	2	4	5	3	0	3	7	6	0	14
11.	West Ham U	11	3	1	2	7	7	1	1	3	4	8	-4	14
12.	Leicester City	11	3	0	3	6	9	1	2	2	3	4	-4	14
13.	Middlesbrough	11	2	2	2	11	9	1	2	2	5	9	-2	13
14.	Sunderland	11	2	3	1	5	4	1	1	3	4	7	-2	13
15.	Southampton	11	3	2	1	15	6	0	1	4	5	10	+4	12
16.	Derby County	11	1	2	2	5	7	1	3	2	5	7	-4	11
17.	Leeds Utd	11	2	0	3	3	7	1	1	4	5	11	-10	10
18.	Nottingham F	11	0	3	3	3	9	1	2	2	7	9	-8	8
19.	Coventry City	11	1	3	2	3	6	0	2	3	1	8	-10	8
20.	Blackburn R	11	0	1	4	2	8	0	3	3	5	8	-9	4

F. A. Carling Premiership
League Table—30 November 1996

				HOME					AWAY					
		Plyd	*W*	*D*	*L*	*For*	*Agt*	*W*	*D*	*L*	*For*	*Agt*	*GD*	*Pts*
1.	Arsenal	15	5	2	0	17	5	4	2	2	12	8	+16	31
2.	Newcastle Utd	15	5	1	2	19	10	4	1	2	7	7	+9	29
3.	Liverpool	14	4	3	0	13	5	4	1	2	11	8	+11	28
4.	Wimbledon	15	5	2	1	17	10	3	2	2	9	6	+10	28
5.	Manchester U	15	5	2	1	16	8	2	3	2	13	14	+7	26
6.	Chelsea	14	3	3	1	11	8	3	3	1	12	11	+4	24
7.	Aston Villa	15	5	2	1	11	5	2	1	4	8	10	+4	24
8.	Everton	15	4	1	3	16	9	2	4	1	7	9	+5	23
9.	Derby County	15	4	2	2	11	9	1	4	2	6	8	0	21
10.	Sheffield Wed	15	3	4	1	8	6	2	2	3	8	12	-2	21
11.	Tottenham H	14	3	2	2	7	5	3	0	4	8	9	+1	20
12.	Sunderland	15	2	4	1	6	5	2	1	5	7	13	-5	17
13.	West Ham U	15	3	2	2	8	8	1	3	4	5	10	-5	17
14.	Leicester City	15	3	0	4	7	11	2	2	4	7	10	-7	17
15.	Leeds Utd	14	3	0	4	6	9	2	1	4	7	11	-7	16
16.	Middlesbrough	15	2	3	2	13	11	1	2	5	7	15	-6	14
17.	Southampton	15	3	2	2	15	8	0	2	6	8	20	-5	13
18.	Blackburn R	15	2	2	4	8	10	0	4	3	7	10	-5	12
19.	Coventry City	15	1	3	3	4	8	0	4	4	5	13	-12	10
20.	Nottingham F	15	0	4	3	5	11	1	2	5	7	14	-13	9

F. A. Carling Premiership
League Table—31 December 1996

		Plyd	W	D	L	For	Agt	W	D	L	For	Agt	GD	Pts
			HOME					*AWAY*						
1.	Liverpool	21	6	4	1	23	10	6	2	2	15	9	+19	42
2.	Manchester U	20	7	2	1	22	8	3	5	2	20	17	+17	37
3.	Arsenal	20	6	4	0	24	10	4	3	3	13	10	+17	37
4.	Wimbledon	19	6	2	1	18	10	5	2	3	15	13	+10	37
5.	Newcastle Utd	20	6	2	2	27	12	4	2	4	8	10	+13	34
6.	Aston Villa	20	6	2	2	16	7	4	2	4	13	12	+10	34
7.	Chelsea	20	4	5	1	18	13	4	3	3	14	16	+3	32
8.	Everton	20	4	2	4	17	12	3	5	2	12	15	+2	28
9.	Sheffield Wed	20	3	6	1	9	7	3	4	3	12	15	-1	28
10.	Tottenham H	20	4	3	3	11	9	4	1	5	11	17	-4	28
11.	Derby County	20	4	3	3	11	10	1	5	4	9	15	-5	23
12.	Leicester City	20	3	2	5	10	16	3	3	4	10	11	-7	23
13.	Sunderland	20	4	4	2	12	8	2	1	7	7	20	-9	23
14.	Coventry City	20	3	3	4	10	11	2	4	4	10	14	-5	22
15.	Leeds Utd	20	4	1	5	9	12	2	3	5	7	12	-8	22
16.	West Ham U	19	4	3	3	12	12	1	3	5	6	13	-7	21
17.	Middlesbrough	20	3	4	3	17	15	1	2	7	8	23	-13	18
18.	Blackburn R	19	3	2	4	9	10	0	6	4	8	12	-5	17
19.	Southampton	20	4	2	4	18	11	0	2	8	10	26	-9	16
20.	Nottingham F	20	1	5	4	7	16	1	3	6	11	20	-18	14

F. A. Carling Premiership
League Table—31 January 1997

		Plyd	HOME					AWAY					GD	Pts
			W	D	L	For	Agt	W	D	L	For	Agt		
1.	Manchester U	24	8	3	1	24	9	5	5	2	24	18	+21	47
2.	Arsenal	24	8	4	0	29	11	5	3	4	15	12	+21	46
3.	Liverpool	24	7	5	1	26	10	6	2	3	15	10	+21	46
4.	Newcastle Utd	24	8	2	2	34	13	4	4	4	12	14	+19	42
5.	Wimbledon	22	6	3	1	19	11	5	2	5	16	16	+8	38
6.	Chelsea	23	6	5	1	22	14	4	3	4	14	18	+4	38
7.	Aston Villa	24	6	3	3	18	10	4	3	5	13	15	+6	36
8.	Sheffield Wed	23	4	6	1	11	8	4	4	4	15	19	-1	34
9.	Tottenham H	23	5	3	4	14	12	4	1	6	12	19	-5	31
10.	Leeds Utd	24	5	2	5	12	12	3	3	6	9	15	-6	29
11.	Sunderland	24	5	5	2	13	8	2	3	7	10	23	-8	29
12.	Everton	24	4	2	5	17	14	3	5	5	15	24	-6	28
13.	Leicester City	23	4	3	5	12	17	3	3	5	10	14	-9	27
14.	Coventry City	24	3	4	5	12	15	3	4	5	11	18	-10	26
15.	Derby County	23	4	3	3	11	10	1	7	5	11	19	-7	25
16.	Blackburn R	23	4	2	4	13	10	1	7	5	11	14	0	24
17.	Nottingham F	24	3	5	5	11	18	2	3	6	12	20	-15	23
18.	West Ham U	23	4	3	6	13	17	1	4	5	6	13	-11	22
19.	Middlesbrough	23	4	4	4	21	18	1	2	8	8	25	-14	21
20.	Southampton	22	4	3	4	20	13	1	2	8	11	26	-8	20

F. A. Carling Premiership
League Table—28 February 1997

		Plyd	W	D	L	For	Agt	W	D	L	For	Agt	GD	Pts
			HOME					*AWAY*						
1.	Manchester U	27	9	3	1	26	10	6	6	2	27	20	+23	54
2.	Liverpool	27	8	6	1	30	10	7	2	3	16	10	+26	53
3.	Newcastle Utd	26	9	2	2	38	16	5	4	4	13	14	+21	48
4.	Arsenal	28	8	4	2	30	14	5	5	4	15	12	+19	48
5.	Wimbledon	25	6	4	1	20	12	6	3	5	17	16	+9	43
6.	Aston Villa	27	8	3	3	21	11	4	4	5	13	15	+8	43
7.	Chelsea	25	6	6	1	23	15	5	3	4	16	19	+5	42
8.	Sheffield Wed	26	4	7	1	11	8	5	5	4	20	23	0	39
9.	Leeds Utd	27	5	3	5	12	12	4	3	7	10	19	-9	33
10.	Everton	26	5	2	5	19	14	3	6	5	15	24	-4	32
11.	Tottenham H	26	5	4	5	15	14	4	1	7	15	23	-7	32
12.	Leicester City	25	5	3	5	16	19	3	3	6	13	18	-8	30
13.	Derby County	27	5	4	4	14	13	1	7	6	13	23	-9	29
14.	Sunderland	26	5	5	3	13	9	2	3	8	10	24	-10	29
15.	Blackburn R	25	5	2	4	15	11	1	8	5	11	14	+1	28
16.	Coventry City	27	3	5	5	12	15	3	5	6	12	20	-11	28
17.	West Ham U	26	5	3	6	17	20	1	4	7	7	16	-12	25
18.	Nottingham F	26	3	6	5	11	18	2	3	7	12	22	-17	24
19.	Middlesbrough	25	4	4	5	21	19	1	3	8	9	26	-15	22
20.	Southampton	25	4	4	5	22	16	1	2	9	12	28	-10	21

F. A. Carling Premiership
League Table—31 March 1997

		Plyd	HOME					AWAY					GD	Pts
			W	D	L	For	Agt	W	D	L	For	Agt		
1.	Manchester U	31	11	3	1	31	11	7	6	3	30	22	+28	63
2.	Liverpool	31	9	6	1	34	13	8	3	4	19	13	+27	60
3.	Arsenal	32	9	4	3	33	16	7	5	4	19	12	+24	57
4.	Newcastle Utd	30	10	2	3	42	17	5	5	5	17	19	+23	52
5.	Aston Villa	31	9	4	3	22	11	5	4	6	15	16	+10	50
6.	Chelsea	31	8	7	1	31	18	5	3	7	20	26	+7	49
7.	Sheffield Wed	31	6	8	1	18	12	6	5	5	23	25	+4	49
8.	Wimbledon	30	6	6	2	23	17	6	4	6	19	20	+5	46
9.	Leeds Utd	32	7	4	5	14	12	4	4	8	12	22	-8	41
10.	Tottenham H	31	6	4	6	16	15	5	2	8	22	28	-5	39
11.	Leicester City	31	6	4	6	19	23	4	5	6	18	21	-7	39
12.	Blackburn R	31	7	3	5	20	15	1	9	6	13	17	+1	36
13.	Everton	31	6	2	7	20	18	3	7	6	17	27	-8	36
14.	Middlesbrough	31	7	5	5	31	22	2	3	9	13	30	-8	35
15.	Derby County	31	7	4	4	21	17	1	7	8	14	30	-12	35
16.	West Ham U	31	6	3	6	20	22	2	6	8	11	19	-10	33
17.	Sunderland	32	6	6	4	16	15	2	3	11	13	33	-19	33
18.	Nottingham F	33	3	7	6	12	22	3	6	8	16	27	-21	31
19.	Coventry City	32	3	7	6	14	19	3	5	8	13	27	-19	30
20.	Southampton	31	4	6	6	26	22	2	3	10	13	29	-12	27

F. A. Carling Premiership
League Table—30 April 1997

		Plyd	HOME					AWAY					GD	Pts
			W	D	L	For	Agt	W	D	L	For	Agt		
1.	Manchester U	34	11	3	2	33	14	9	6	3	36	25	+30	69
2.	Arsenal	36	10	5	3	36	17	8	6	4	23	13	+29	65
3.	Liverpool	35	9	6	3	36	18	9	4	4	22	15	+25	64
4.	Newcastle Utd	34	12	3	3	49	20	5	6	5	18	20	+27	60
5.	Aston Villa	36	10	5	3	26	13	6	5	7	18	18	+13	58
6.	Sheffield Wed	35	8	9	1	24	15	6	5	6	24	29	+4	56
7.	Chelsea	36	9	7	2	33	22	6	3	9	23	32	+2	55
8.	Wimbledon	35	7	6	4	25	20	6	4	8	20	24	+1	49
9.	Tottenham H	36	8	4	6	18	15	5	3	10	24	32	-5	46
10.	Leeds Utd	36	7	6	5	14	12	4	5	9	13	25	-10	44
11.	Derby County	36	8	6	4	24	19	2	7	9	18	35	-12	43
12.	Everton	36	7	4	7	23	20	3	8	7	20	32	-9	42
13.	Blackburn R	35	8	3	6	26	19	1	11	6	14	18	+3	41
14.	Leicester City	35	6	4	7	19	24	4	6	8	20	26	-11	40
15.	Southampton	36	5	7	6	30	24	4	4	10	18	31	-7	38
16.	West Ham U	35	6	5	6	22	24	3	6	9	12	21	-11	38
17.	Coventry City	36	4	8	6	18	21	4	6	8	17	30	-16	38
18.	Sunderland	36	6	6	6	17	18	3	4	11	15	34	-20	37
19.	Middlesbrough	34	7	5	6	31	23	2	4	10	13	31	-10	36
20.	Nottingham F	36	3	8	7	14	26	3	7	8	16	27	-23	33

F. A. Carling Premiership
Final League Positions—12 May 1997

		Plyd	W	D	L	For	Agt	W	D	L	For	Agt	GD	Pts
			HOME					*AWAY*						
1.	Manchester U	38	12	5	2	38	17	9	7	3	38	27	+32	75
2.	Newcastle Utd	38	13	3	3	54	20	6	8	5	19	20	+33	68
3.	Arsenal	38	10	5	4	36	18	9	6	4	26	14	+30	68
4.	Liverpool	38	10	6	3	38	19	9	5	5	24	18	+25	68
5.	Aston Villa	38	11	5	3	27	13	6	5	8	20	21	+13	61
6.	Chelsea	38	9	8	2	33	22	7	3	9	25	33	+3	59
7.	Sheffield Wed	38	8	10	1	25	16	6	5	8	25	35	-1	57
8.	Wimbledon	38	9	6	4	28	21	6	5	8	21	25	+3	56
9.	Leicester City	38	7	5	7	22	26	5	6	8	24	28	-8	47
10.	Tottenham H	38	8	4	7	19	17	5	3	11	25	34	-7	46
11.	Leeds Utd	38	7	7	5	15	13	4	6	9	13	25	-10	46
12.	Derby County	38	8	6	5	25	22	3	7	9	20	36	-13	46
13.	Blackburn R	38	8	4	7	28	23	1	11	7	14	20	-1	42
14.	West Ham U	38	7	6	6	27	25	3	6	10	12	23	-9	42
15.	Everton	38	7	4	8	24	22	3	8	8	20	35	-13	42
16.	Southampton	38	6	7	6	32	24	4	4	11	18	32	-6	41
17.	Coventry City	38	4	8	7	19	23	5	6	8	19	31	-16	41
18.	Sunderland	38	7	6	6	20	18	3	4	12	15	35	-18	40
19.	Middlesbrough	38	8	5	6	34	25	2	7	10	17	35	-9	39 *
20.	Nottingham F	38	3	9	7	15	27	3	7	9	16	32	-28	34

* Middlesbrough deducted 3 points

APPENDIX B

1996/97 Season
Carling Premiership League
Results

HOME \ AWAY	Arsenal	Aston Villa	Blackburn R	Chelsea	Coventry C	Derby County	Everton	Leeds Utd	Leicester C
Arsenal	-	2-2	1-1	3-3	0-0	2-2	3-1	3-0	2-0
Aston Villa	2-2	-	1-0	0-2	2-1	2-0	3-1	2-0	1-3
Blackburn R	0-2	0-2	-	1-1	4-0	1-2	1-1	0-1	2-4
Chelsea	0-3	1-1	1-1	-	2-0	3-1	2-2	0-0	2-1
Coventry C	1-1	1-2	0-0	3-1	-	1-2	0-0	2-1	0-0
Derby County	1-3	2-1	0-0	3-2	2-1	-	0-1	3-3	2-0
Everton	0-2	0-1	0-2	1-2	1-1	1-0	-	0-0	1-1
Leeds Utd	0-0	0-0	0-0	2-0	1-3	0-0	1-0	-	3-0
Leicester C	0-2	1-0	1-1	1-3	0-2	4-2	1-2	1-0	-
Liverpool	2-0	3-0	0-0	5-1	1-2	2-1	1-1	4-0	1-1
Man Utd	1-0	0-0	2-2	1-2	3-1	2-3	2-2	1-0	3-1
Middlesboro'	0-2	3-2	2-1	1-0	4-0	6-1	4-2	0-0	0-2
Newcastle U	1-2	4-3	2-1	3-1	4-0	3-1	4-1	3-0	4-3
Nott'm F	2-1	0-0	2-2	2-0	0-1	1-1	0-1	1-1	0-0
Sheff Wed	0-0	2-1	1-1	0-2	0-0	0-0	2-1	2-2	2-1
Southampton	0-2	0-1	2-0	0-0	2-2	3-1	2-2	0-2	2-2
Sunderland	1-0	1-0	0-0	3-0	1-0	2-0	3-0	0-1	0-0
Tottenham H	0-0	1-0	2-1	1-2	1-2	1-1	0-0	1-0	1-2
West Ham U	1-2	0-2	2-1	3-2	1-1	1-1	2-2	0-2	1-0
Wimbledon	2-2	0-2	1-0	0-1	2-2	1-1	4-0	2-0	1-3

	Liverpool	Man Utd	Middlesboro'	Newcastle U	Nott'm F	Sheff Wed	Southampton	Sunderland	Tottenham H	West Ham U	Wimbledon
	1-2	1-2	2-0	0-1	2-0	4-1	3-1	2-0	3-1	2-0	0-1
	1-0	0-0	1-0	2-2	2-0	0-1	1-0	1-0	1-1	0-0	5-0
	3-0	2-3	0-0	1-0	1-1	4-1	2-1	1-0	0-2	2-1	3-i
	1-0	1-1	1-0	1-1	1-1	2-2	1-0	6-2	3-1	3-1	2-4
	0-1	0-2	3-0	2-1	0-3	0-0	1-1	2-2	1-2	1-3	1-1
	0-1	1-1	2-1	0-1	0-0	2-2	1-1	1-0	4-2	1-0	0-2
	1-1	0-2	1-2	2-0	2-0	2-0	7-1	1-3	1-0	2-1	1-3
	0-2	0-4	1-1	0-1	2-0	0-2	0-0	3-0	0-0	1-0	1-0
	0-3	2-2	1-3	2-0	2-2	1-0	2-1	1-1	1-1	0-1	1-0
	-	1-3	5-1	4-3	4-2	0-1	2-1	0-0	2-1	0-0	1-1
	1-0	-	3-3	0-0	4-1	2-0	2-1	5-0	2-0	2-0	2-1
	3-3	2-2	-	0-1	1-1	4-2	0-1	0-1	0-3	4-1	0-0
	1-1	5-0	3-1	-	5-0	1-2	0-1	1-1	7-1	1-1	2-0
	1-1	0-4	1-1	0-0	-	0-3	1-3	1-4	2-1	0-2	1-1
	1-1	1-1	3-1	1-1	2-0	-	1-1	2-1	2-1	0-0	3-1
	0-1	6-3	4-0	2-2	2-2	2-3	-	3-0	0-1	2-0	0-0
	1-2	2-1	2-2	1-2	1-1	1-1	0-1	-	0-4	0-0	1-3
	0-?	1-?	1-0	1-?	0-1	1-1	3-1	2-0	-	1-0	1-0
	1-2	2-2	0-0	0-0	0-1	5-1	2-1	2-0	4-3	-	0-2
	2-1	0-3	1-1	1-1	1-0	4-2	3-1	1-0	1-0	1-1	-

APPENDIX C

1996/97 Season
Everton F. C. and Wales
Results—Month by Month

AUGUST

17	**Everton**	2 - 0	Newcastle United
21	Manchester U	2 - 2	**Everton**
24	Tottenham H	0 - 0	**Everton**
31	**Wales**	6 - 0	San Marino

SEPTEMBER

4	**Everton**	0 - 1	Aston Villa
7	Wimbledon	4 - 0	**Everton**
14	**Everton**	1 - 2	Middlesbrough
18	**Everton**	1 - 1	York City
21	Blackburn R	1 - 1	**Everton**
24	York City	3 - 2	**Everton**
28	**Everton**	2 - 0	Sheffield Wednesday

OCTOBER

5	**Wales**	1 - 3	Holland
12	**Everton**	2 - 1	West Ham
21	Liverpool	v	**Everton**—*match postponed*
28	Nott'm F	0 - 1	**Everton**

NOVEMBER

4	**Everton**	1 - 1	Coventry City
9	Holland	7 - 1	**Wales**
16	**Everton**	7 - 1	Southampton
20	Liverpool	1 - 1	**Everton**
23	Leicester City	1 - 2	**Everton**
30	**Everton**	1 - 3	Sunderland

DECEMBER

7	Chelsea	2 - 2	**Everton**
14	**Wales**	0 - 0	Turkey
16	Derby County	0 - 1	**Everton**
21	**Everton**	0 - 0	Leeds United

| 26 | Middlesboro' | 4 - 2 | **Everton** |
| 28 | **Everton** | 1 - 3 | Wimbledon |

JANUARY

1	**Everton**	0 - 2	Blackburn Rovers
5	**Everton**	3 - 0	Swindon Town
11	Sheffield Wed	2 - 1	**Everton**
19	Arsenal	3 - 1	**Everton**
25	**Everton**	2 - 3	Bradford City
29	Newcastle U	4 - 1	**Everton**

FEBRUARY

1	**Everton**	2 - 0	Nottingham Forest
11	**Wales**	0 - 0	Republic of Ireland
22	Coventry City	0 - 0	**Everton**

MARCH

1	**Everton**	0 - 2	Arsenal
5	Southampton	2 - 2	**Everton**
8	Leeds United	1 - 0	**Everton**
15	**Everton**	1 - 0	Derby County
22	**Everton**	0 - 2	Manchester United
29	**Wales**	1 - 2	Belgium

APRIL

5	Aston Villa	3 - 1	**Everton**
9	**Everton**	1 - 1	Leicester City
12	**Everton**	1 - 0	Tottenham Hotspur
16	**Everton**	1 - 1	Liverpool
19	West Ham	2 - 2	**Everton**

MAY

| 3 | Sunderland | 3 - 0 | **Everton** |
| 11 | **Everton** | 1 - 2 | Chelsea |

APPENDIX D

Neville Southall—
Factfile

BIRTHPLACE:	Llandudno, Wales
BIRTHDATE:	16th September 1958
HEIGHT:	6' 1"
WEIGHT:	14st 7lb

CLUBS PLAYED FOR:
Winsford United, Bury, Port Vale (on loan), Everton.

PREVIOUS JOBS:
Labourer, chef, hod-carrier, binman, and hod carrier again.

HONOURS:
Two League Championships (1985, 1987), two FA Cups (1984, 1995), one European Cup Winner's Cup (1985) and one Football Writers' Footballer of the Year award (1985).

EVERTON DEBUT:
Against Ipswich on October 17th 1981 in a 2-1 victory at Goodison Park.

WALES DEBUT:
Against Northern Ireland at Wrexham on May 27th 1982. Wales won 3-0.

GREATEST SAVE:
Against Tottenham's Mark Falco at White Hart Lane in 1985. It helped us win a crucial league match and we went on to become champions.

GOALS SCORED:
One. In a penalty shoot-out against Charlton in a Full Members cup-tie at Goodison Park.